CLANS AND FAMILIES OF IRELAND

Designed by Philip Clucas
Edited by David Gibbon
Heraldic Artwork by Myra Maguire
Featuring the Photography of Neil Sutherland
and Michael Diggin

for Breda

Published by
THE WELLFLEET PRESS
A Division of **BOOK SALES, INC.**
110 Enterprise Avenue
Secaucus, New Jersey 07094
CLB 2938
Reprinted in 1994
© 1993 CLB Publishing Ltd., Godalming, Surrey, England
Printed and bound in Hong Kong by Sing Cheong
All rights reserved
ISBN 1-55521-887-3

CLANS AND FAMILIES OF IRELAND

THE HERITAGE AND HERALDRY OF IRISH CLANS AND FAMILIES

JOHN GRENHAM

THE WELLFLEET PRESS
WELLFLEET

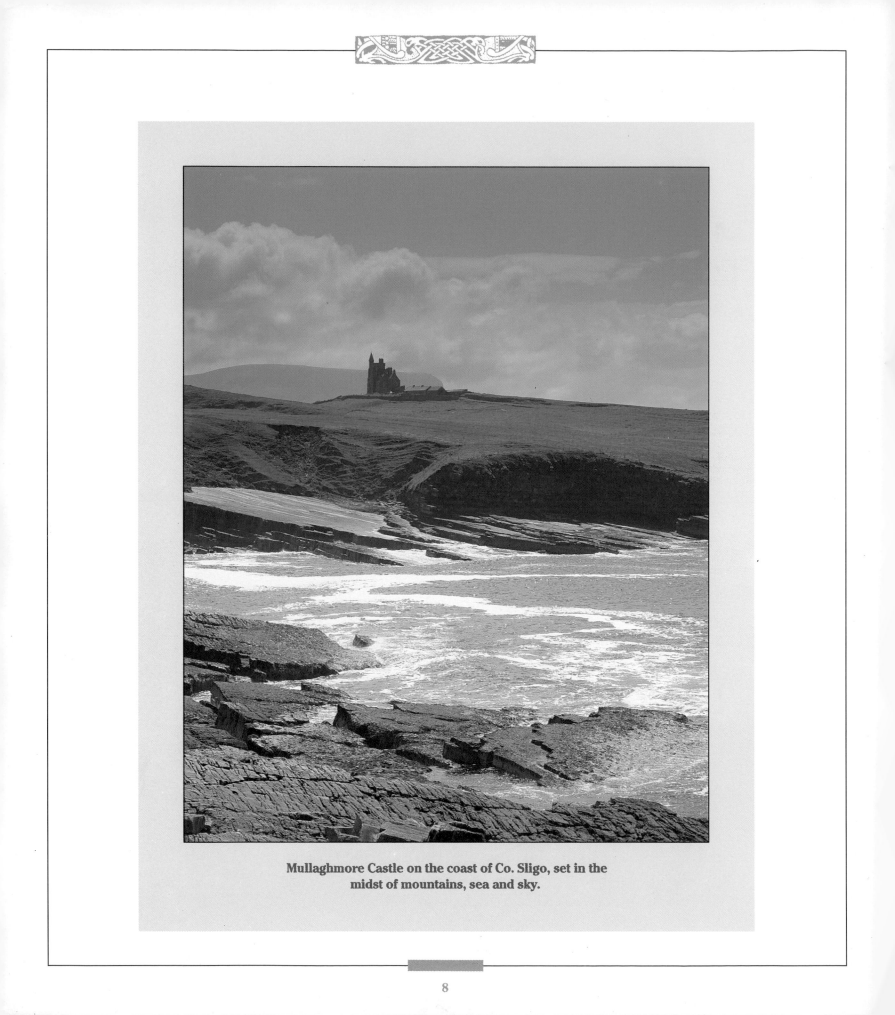

Mullaghmore Castle on the coast of Co. Sligo, set in the
midst of mountains, sea and sky.

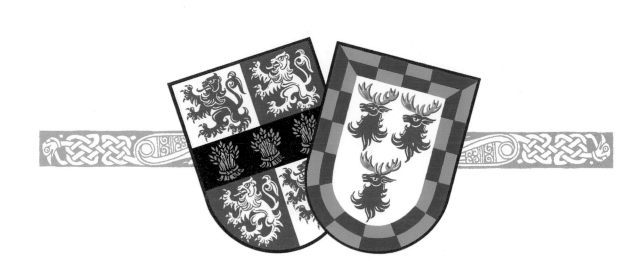

Contents

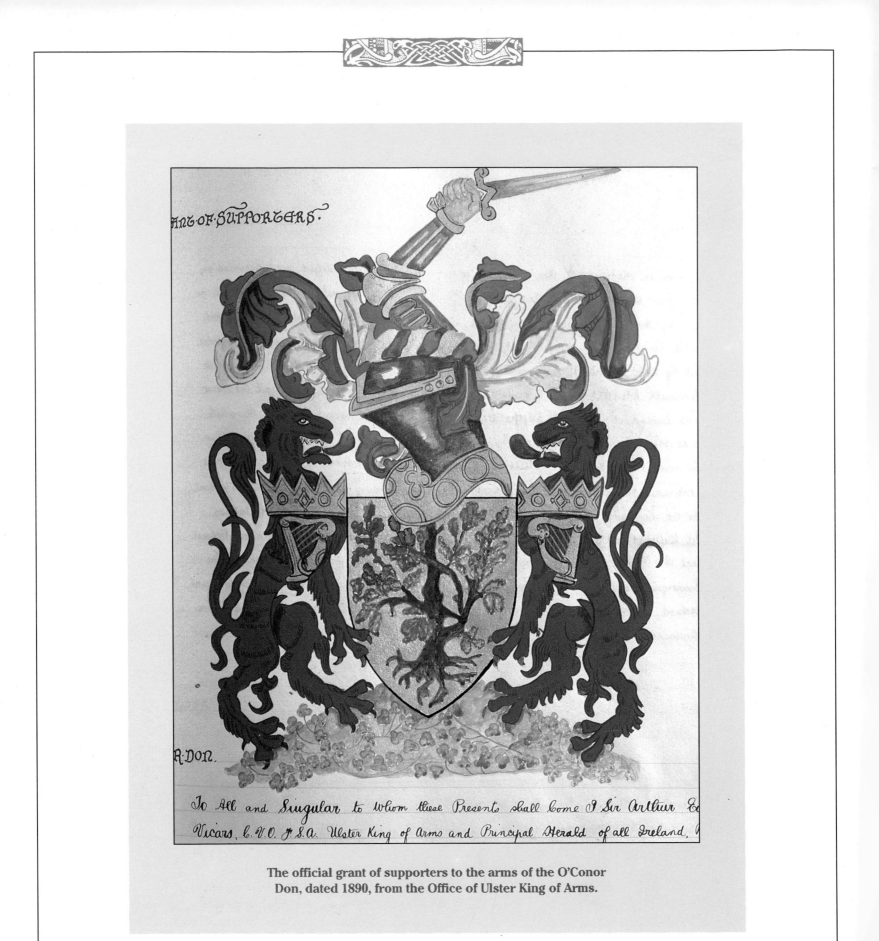

The official grant of supporters to the arms of the O'Conor Don, dated 1890, from the Office of Ulster King of Arms.

Foreword

The system of hereditary surnames currently in use in Ireland developed over the past thousand years and some of the oldest surnames in any country in Europe can be found recorded in Irish annals. During the eleventh and twelfth centuries there emerged a number of powerful families out of the tribal milieu of Gaelic Ireland, each with a fixed surname invariably derived from an immediate ancestor of consequence. The possession of an hereditary surname readily identified the head of a ruling family and its adherents, and was therefore often a considerable political asset.

The great wealth of territorial, personal and family names so characteristic of Irish culture is due to the influx of numerous peoples into the island of Ireland in historic and indeed prehistoric times. Naturally, each of these peoples brought with them their own language, be that Gaelic, Welsh, Norse, Norman-French or English, and these languages determined to a large measure the future shape and form of surnames in Ireland. The multiplicity of variants in the same surname is accounted for by the anglicization process, which began to have effect in Ireland from the eighteenth century onwards.

The author has compiled his material carefully and presents it in an easy and direct style. The text is neatly complemented throughout with a variety of appropriate illustrations, resulting in a rounded and colourful production. The publication of this book will be welcomed by Irish people at home and abroad and will contribute significantly to a greater understanding and appreciation of the history of Irish families, their surnames and the ancient heraldic symbols associated with them.

Donal Begley

Donal Begley
The Chief Herald of Ireland

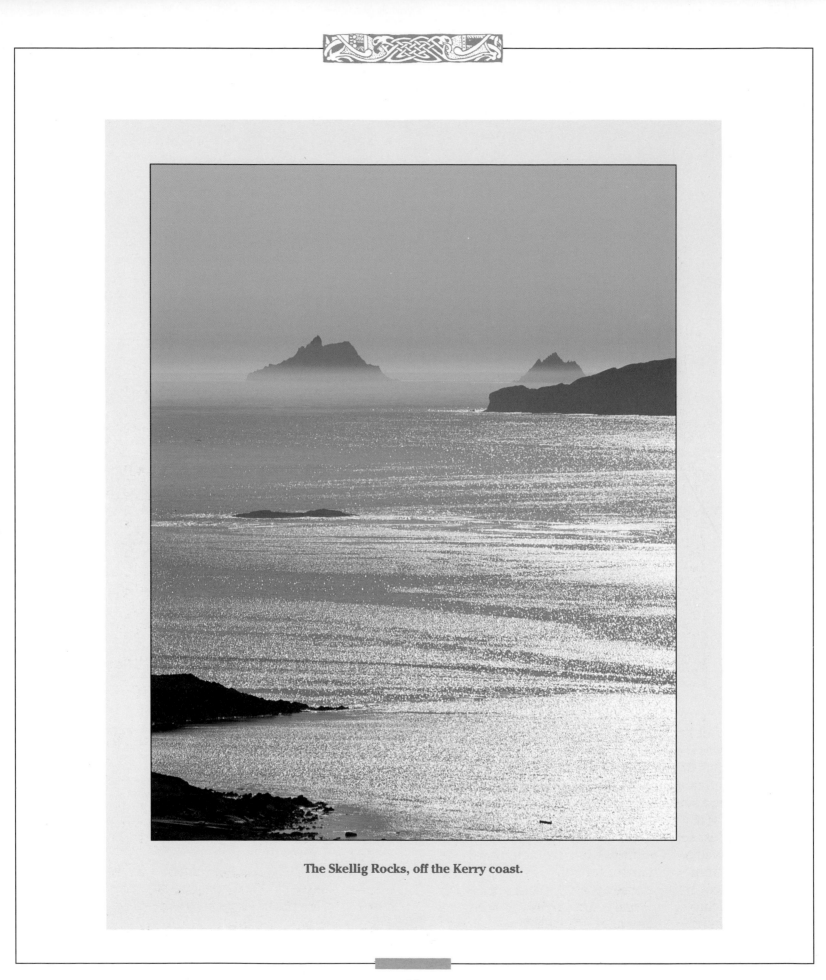

The Skellig Rocks, off the Kerry coast.

Clans and Families of Ireland

The Earliest Peoples and the Celts

Until about 12,000 B.C. Ireland, like the rest of northern Europe, was still in the grip of the Ice Age and was joined physically, with Britain, to the Continent. Only when the ice had retreated and the seas risen, about 8,000 B.C., did it become a separate island, separated from the British peninsula (as it then was) by the narrow North Channel. The earliest settlers, the Mesolithic people, appear to have arrived at about this period, migrating across the Channel from Scotland into northern Ireland. The island was still covered in dense woods, and the new arrivals travelled through it by water, living by fishing, and dwelt on lake and river shores and by the sea. Traces of them

Poulnabrone Dolmen, Co. Clare, the classic skeleton of a Neolithic tomb.

are found today, principally in the north, though some evidence of their way of life has been found as far south as Carlow.

The first firm knowledge of our early forebears, however, comes with the arrival of the Neolithic peoples, about 3,500 B.C. These were the first farmers, growing crops, domesticating animals, using more sophisticated

stone tools than their predecessors. It was at this period that the clearance of the thick forest covering most of the country began. Over the following 3,000 years a whole succession of colonizing invasions took place, bringing with them mature cultures and societies, evidence of which is still visible in the Irish countryside today. Thousands of megalithic tombs (literally 'built with great stones') are still to be found throughout the country, the most famous being Newgrange, over 40 feet high and covering more than an acre, oriented so that sunlight penetrates to the inner chamber only on the days of the winter and summer solstices. The social complexity and planning required to create such elaborate structures is clear, and those who built them must have had sophisticated laws, religion and societies.

The first impact of Newgrange (this page and facing page bottom) is its sheer size, but the elaborately detailed and mysterious decoration is equally impressive. Other structures, such as Drombeg stone circle in Co. Cork (facing page top), are smaller and simpler, but no less mute regarding their origins.

Without a written language, however, their history is lost to us, apart from the silent evidence of their monuments. From these we can see that they were expert miners, metalworkers, builders, and traders – a rich mixture of peoples and cultures covering more than twenty centuries.

The Celts

About the year 600 B.C. came the first of the peoples who were to determine the character of the country for the next two millennia. These were the Celts, who brought with them complex, clearly defined laws and religion, expertise in making iron and weapons, a warrior tradition and strong tribal networks. As with earlier Neolithic invaders, the newcomers did not simply replace the earlier inhabitants. Even where one culture became dominant, as did Celtic, the descendants of the earlier peoples remained, adapting and assimilating. The *Lebor Gabhála* or 'Book of Invasions', written in the ninth century A.D. but drawing on much earlier traditions, is the first account of the arrival of the Celts. Although much of it is undoubtedly mythological, nonetheless with its aid it is possible tentatively to distinguish four

separate waves of Celtic settlement in the six centuries before Christ.

The first of these peoples were known as 'Pretani', and later called *Cruithnigh* by the Irish annalists. They were firmly established in the country before 500 B.C. and appear to have made their way into eastern Ulster from Scotland. To the Romans, these were the tribes later known as Picts. In Ireland, their descendants were the Dál Riada tribes, dominating north eastern Ulster up to the ninth and tenth centuries A.D. More extensive evidence has survived about the second wave of Celtic settlement. The new peoples called themselves *Euerni*, a name written later by the annalists as *Érainn*. Their new home they called after themselves, *Eueriio*. For the Greek and Roman cartographers, this became *Ierin* and *Iouernia*, and from this latter was eventually derived the Latin name for the country, Hibernia. The modern Irish name for the island evolved more directly, from the Celtic *Eueriio* through the Old Irish *Ériu* to *Éire*; from *Éire* came 'Ireland', through the simple addition of the English suffix '-land'.

The earliest map of Ireland, drawn in the second century A.D. by Claudius Ptolemy of Alexandria, shows branches of the *Érainn* widely spread throughout the country, but it is with the south that they appear to have had the strongest connection. Ptolemy locates the *Iverni*, treated as a single tribe, in the present county of Cork, and subsequent research has identified several sub-tribes in the area. From these tribes have come some of the oldest place names in the country – the *Ciarraige* giving their name to modern Kerry, the *Fir Máige* to the town and barony of Fermoy in Co. Cork, the *Uí Bairche* (or *Brigantes* in Ptolemy's map) to the barony of Bargy in south Wexford.

From the strength of the associations of the *Érainn* with the south of the country, it is reasonable to suppose that it was in the south that they first established themselves, probably in the fifth century B.C., afterwards extending their conquest to the rest of the island. This view is reinforced by evidence which suggests that the

Ogham stones (above right) record the earliest memorial inscriptions in Ireland. Prehistoric forts such as Dun Aengus on the Aran Islands (bottom right and far right) suggest, through their size and isolation, the scale of the violence they were built to withstand.

Érainn were in fact part of the *Belgae*, the name applied by the Romans to large sections of the Continental Celts. *Bolg*, one of the most common of the Celtic names for their sun-god, was given in the later genealogical tracts as one of the mythical ancestors of these people; the derivation of the name from *Bolgi* (Celtic) to *Belgae* (Latin) and *Fir Bolg* (Irish) is suggestive, at the very least.

The third Celtic wave of colonization took place, it is believed, around the year 300 B.C. These were the *Laighin*, whose name comes from the *laigne*, or spears, with which they armed themselves. From their association from the earliest times with what is now the modern province of Leinster (in Irish *Laighin*), it may be taken that this was the area in which they first landed, coming directly, it is thought, from the western part of Normandy. They extended their power across the island gradually, moving towards the western seaboard, and in the process forcing the *Érainn* or *Fir Bolg* into the remoter parts of the country. Tradition from this period ascribes to the *Érainn* the building of the great stone forts still to be found in many of the most isolated parts of Ireland.

Within a few centuries, Laiginian tribes were well established in many parts of the country, and their names have survived to the present in both placenames and surnames. The modern diocese of Ossory, covering almost all of County Kilkenny, takes its name from the *Osraige*, one of the most prominent of these tribes, while the barony of Idrone in Co. Carlow is the old homeland of the *Uí Drona*. From the *Uí Ceinnselaigh*, a tribe inhabiting parts of south Wexford, comes the modern surname Kinsella, still common in the Wexford area. The spread of the Laiginian peoples is also reflected in the placenames of Mayo, Roscommon and Galway, but it is in south Leinster that their power held out to the tenth century.

The Gaeil

The last of the major Celtic settlements in Ireland took place about the year 50 B.C., and was a direct result of Roman attempts to dominate the Celtic tribes of Gaul. Among the many peoples uprooted and dispersed by this attempt were a group who appear to have been known to themselves as the *Feni*, who came directly from the Continent to Ireland, arriving, according to popular tradition, in south Kerry and the Boyne estuary.

The earlier inhabitants of the country, who resisted fiercely the incursions of the newcomers, called these people the *Gaodhail* or *Gaeil*, from the language they spoke, Gaedelg, in English 'Gaelic'. Although details of the history of the first centuries A.D. remain obscure, it is clear that the influence and power of the *Gaeil* spread steadily over the next three centuries at the expense of the *Laighin* and the *Érainn*, expanding northwards from Kerry into Tipperary and Limerick, and westwards into Roscommon and Galway, until by the fifth century they were dominant throughout most of Ireland and had established the dynasties and tribal groupings which determined the politics and culture of the country until the arrival of the Normans.

As they pushed their way west and north through Ireland, the *Gaeil* also made their presence felt on the western coasts of Britain, where the decline of Roman power left many relatively wealthy areas vulnerable to attack. Sporadic raids carried out during the third century developed into permanent settlements in the fourth and fifth, with the largest and most powerful colonies in southwestern Wales and western Scotland, although Cornwall, Devon, Hampshire and the islands of Man, Orkney and Shetland also show signs of this expansion. The main evidence for it today is the distribution of Ogham stones. These are memorial stones, with the name of the person commemorated inscribed by representing Latin letters with groups of lines set at different angles. Virtually all of the stones found in the British Isles are of Irish origin, and their distribution closely reflects the limits of Gaelic power in Britain.

The most important and enduring distinction within the *Gaeil* was between the southern tribes and those of the north and west. In the south they gave themselves the name *Eoghanacht*, or 'people of Eogan', in honour of their ancestor-deity Eogan (in English 'Owen'), and, about the year 400 A.D founded at Cashel the dynasty which held power through most of the southern part of the country from the fifth to the twelfth centuries. In later historical times, the powerful Munster families of O'Sullivan, McCarthy and O'Connell can claim descent from the *Eoghanacht*.

Similarly, in the midlands, west and north, the tribes of the *Gaeil* were known as *Connachta*, or 'people of Conn', in myth the brother of Eogan. Their name endures in the modern province of Connacht. By far the most important of the *Connachta* tribes were the *Uí Néill*,

The notches along the edges of Ogham stones represent letters of the Roman alphabet. Apart from Ireland, they are found only along the west coast of Britain, in areas of Irish colonization.

('O'Neill') claiming descent from Niall Noigiallach ('Niall of the Nine Hostages'), who appears to have lived in the early fifth century, and is given in the genealogical tracts as a son of Eochu Mugmedon ('lord of slaves'), himself several generations descended from Conn. Among Niall's brothers were Ailill, Brion, and Fiachra, founders of the important *Connachta* tribes of *Uí Ailella*, *Uí Briain*, and *Uí Fiachrach*.

The rise of the *Uí Néill* took place through the fifth and sixth centuries, with the conquest of a line of kingdoms stretching from Sligo Bay on the west coast, north to Inishowen in Donegal, and eastwards as far as the Irish Sea. Separate dynasties emerged in the northern and eastern kingdoms, to be known by the later annalists as the northern and southern *Uí Néill*, the former with

their seat at Aileach in Inishowen, the latter based at Tara in County Meath. From the beginning of the seventh century, the *Uí Néill* claimed the high-kingship of all Ireland, alternating between the northern and southern branches. The claim was never accepted by all the other local dynasties, in particular by the *Eoghanacht*, dominant in the southern part of the island, but no serious challenge to the power of the *Uí Néill* emerged until the tenth century.

Although the *Eoghanacht* and the *Uí Néill* were the two predominant tribal groupings, a number of others were locally powerful, particularly in the northeast of the country, where the *Oirialla* controlled territory now included in counties Tyrone, Armagh, Fermanagh and Monaghan, and the *Ulaidh* inhabited what is now counties Down and Antrim. These peoples almost certainly originally possessed lands further to the west, but were displaced by the aggressive expansion to the north and east of the *Uí Néill*.

Gaelic Society

Within these large areas many smaller divisions existed, known as *tuatha*, of which there were about 150 throughout the country; the names of many of these are reflected today in the names of the baronies which make up the modern counties. Each of these *tuatha* had its own ruler or petty king, who owed allegiance to a more powerful leader, an over-king of three or more *tuatha*, who in turn was subordinate to the king of the province, generally of the *Eoghanacht* or the *Uí Néill*. Such an arrangement was clearly ripe for potential conflict, and continuous warfare between *tuatha*, over-kings and provinces was endemic in Ireland until the end of the Middle Ages.

The tribal culture of the *Gaeil*, like that of all Celts, was highly developed and complex, and dominated life throughout the country for fifteen centuries, until its final collapse in the seventeenth century. In essence, it consisted of a highly codified legal system which regulated relationships within and between classes, families, larger kin-groups, and *tuatha*. Three classes existed: the professionals (*aos dána*), made up of poets, historians, jurists, musicians and, before the arrival of Christianity, druids; the free (*saor aicme*), warriors, owning land and cattle; and the unfree (*daor aicme*), slaves, many of whom were prisoners or the descendants of prisoners taken in war.

Above: Staigue Fort, Co. Kerry and the Grianan of Aileach, Co. Donegal (facing page). The Grianan became the chief seat of the northern *Uí Néill*, whose territory took in counties Derry, Donegal, Tyrone and Armagh.

The professionals were widely honoured and, with the exception of the jurists, travelled freely between the various tribes; it was not until the beginning of the eighteenth century that itinerant poets and musicians finally lost their position and privilege. Amongst the free, rights and responsibilities pivoted on the *fine*, or kin-group. For most purposes, this consisted of men who had a great-grandfather in common, that is, up to and including second cousins. Each member of this group bore responsibility for the actions, debts and contracts of the other members, and loyalty to the group was the primary social obligation. The immediate family, as we would understand it, was secondary to the *fine*. Thus, kingship of the *tuath* or the province passed from one member of the *fine* to another, rather than necessarily to the eldest male heir. The vivid sense of kinship and mutual obligation engendered by such a system are clearly visible throughout Irish history, and even in Irish society today.

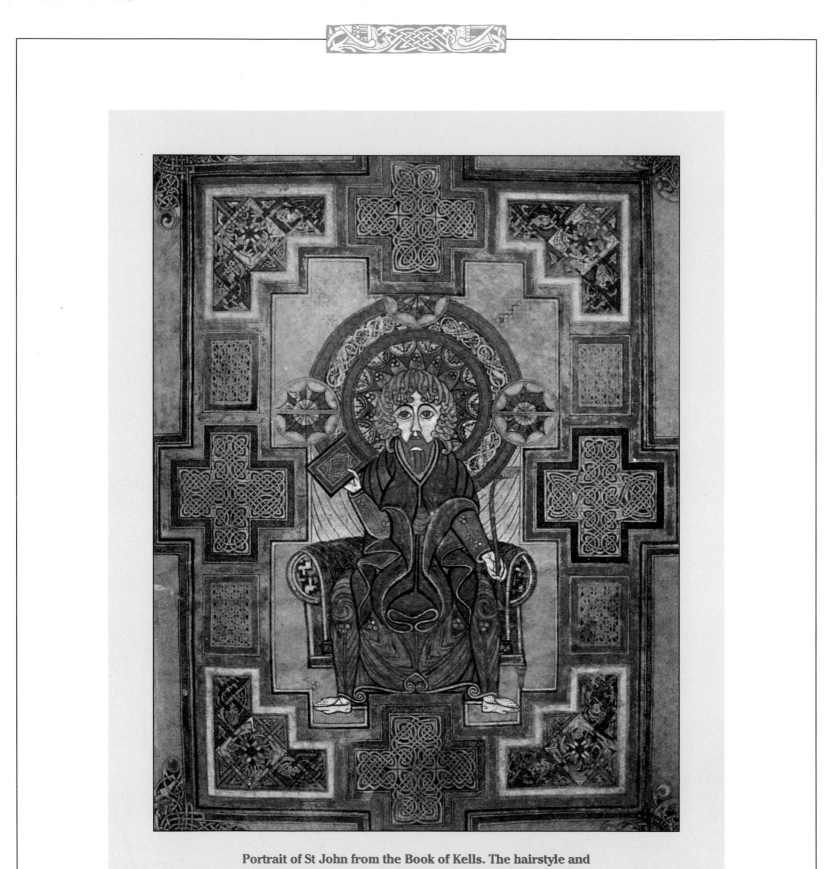

Portrait of St John from the Book of Kells. The hairstyle and
dress are a close reflection of contemporary Irish custom.

Clans and Families of Ireland

Christianity, Placenames and Surnames

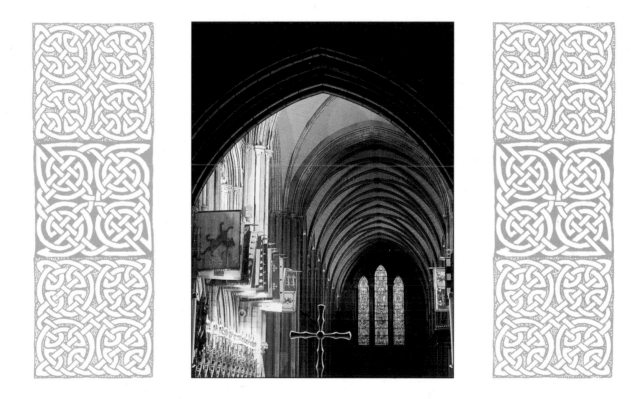

Of all the outside influences on Gaelic culture up to the time of the Tudor conquest, the most powerful was the introduction of Christianity. It was Laoighire, son of Niall Noigiallach and first *Uí Néill* ruler of Tara who reputedly received the Christian missionary Patrick in the year 432; in any case, early missionary activity, largely emanating from Britain, seems to have been concentrated in the northern part of the country, in what was later to be the territory of the *Oirialla*, the *Ulaidh* and the southern *Uí Néill*. Because the earlier pagan religion was tolerant and accommodating, like many polytheistic systems reckoning one god more or

St Patrick's Cathedral, Dublin, dating from 1191, with the banners of the knights of the Order of St Patrick hanging above the choir stalls.

less to be of little importance, Christianity made rapid headway. By the end of the sixth century it was solidly established throughout the country.

In the long term the introduction of Christianity posed problems for Gaelic society; there was simply no place in the existing scheme of things for monastic communities separated from their kin, following a way of life so different from that which surrounded them. In

the end, the solution proved to be that of giving to the most powerful churchmen, bishops and abbots, a status equivalent to that of the king of a *tuath*, with a proportionate status to lower members of the church hierarchy. In turn, the church adapted itself to the existing social structure, and many bishoprics and abbotships remained within the same extended kin-group. As a result, the church in Ireland acquired a large measure of temporal power from an early date.

Above: the ruins of Mellifont Abbey, Co. Louth – the first Cistercian abbey to have been founded in Ireland.

The monks on the bare Atlantic rock of Skellig Michael (left) lived a life of breathtaking austerity and isolation on the very edge of the known world. The High Cross of Kilfenora (above and top) shows how the Vikings influenced the art of the Irish Church, their principal victim.

Monastic ideals very quickly took root as the church grew, with over 800 monasteries founded by the end of the sixth century; abbots soon wielded considerably more power than bishops, as confederations emerged in which a single large monastery might have control of 30 or more smaller establishments. It was this system which provided the closest equivalent in early Ireland to large-scale settlement. Gaelic culture was rural and agricultural, based around the *fine*, and gave rise to no towns. The large monasteries, such as Armagh, Clonmacnoise and Bangor, provided commercial and administrative networks, and were themselves centres of trade, law, and, above all, learning.

It was for this learning, and for their piety, that Irish monks very quickly acquired an international reputation. The copying of manuscript was an important part of the functions of the monasteries, and the sixth and seventh centuries produced such masterpieces of illuminated manuscript as the *Book of Kells* and the *Book of Durrow*, vivid evidence of the monks' extraordinary veneration of learning, and of the rich fusion of Christianity with Celtic tradition.

The security and prosperity of the monasteries at home was the driving force behind the great expansion of Irish influence in Britain and continental Europe between the sixth and tenth centuries. Exile was the ultimate sacrifice for the monks, and it was the quest for such a sacrifice, not missionary fervour, that led so many of them abroad in these years. Once established, however, their fervour and dedication achieved great missionary success, with the conversion of the Picts, and the creation of enduring monastic foundations throughout areas now part of Italy, Austria, Germany, France, Holland, Belgium and Spain, as well as Britain. Even as their fame as religious pioneers and scholars grew, the Irish monks retained many of the distinctive features of their own institutions, for example in refusing to accept the authority of the Pope in calculating the date of Easter. Irish obstinacy was well known; Pope Honorius I wrote to the Irish in 634 'earnestly exhorting them not to think their small number, placed in the utmost borders of the earth, wiser than all the ancient and modern churches of Christ, throughout the world.'

Placenames

The rapid growth of the church is also the source of many of the commonest placenames in Ireland today. For example, two of the most familiar prefixes: 'Kill-', and 'Donagh-', come from Irish words for 'church': *cill* and *domhnach*, the latter meaning literally 'Sunday', and used by extension for the place of worship on that day. Placenames with elements such as these almost invariably originated between the fifth and ninth centuries. Many of the names in everyday use today, in particular those for the smallest geographical unit, the townland, however, are of much greater age, in all probability as old as human habitation itself. This is truest of those names which are derived from natural features, containing such elements as *druim* (Drum-), a height; *cnoc* (Knock-), a hill; *tulach* (Tulla-), a mound; *gleann* (Glen-), a glen. The age of some of these can be gauged from the fact that some of the features they describe no longer exist. Thus 'Derry', in Irish *doire*, meaning 'oakwood', is common and widespread

Facing page bottom: the symbol of the evangelist St Matthew, from the Book of Kells. The heavy walls and strategic situation of many Church settlements, such as those at Kells (facing page top) and on the Rock of Cashel (above), reflect the Church's secular power; Cashel, before becoming the ecclesiastical capital of Munster, had been the seat of the dominant Eoghanacht dynasty for almost six centuries.

throughout the country, even though the forests described in the names have long since vanished.

Of later date, and more fluid, are those names recording human activity: *gort* (Gort-), a field; *baile* (Bally-), place or farm; *ráth* (Rath-), a fort; *lios* (Lis-), an enclosure. In some cases history is itself inscribed in the name: *tamhlacht*, (Tallagh/Tamlaght), means 'famine grave', evidence that famine was familiar in the country from the earliest times. Such names as these proliferated as the population increased, changing and adapting to the different uses made of the land. It was not until the seventeenth century that the demands of the English administrative and legal systems began to enforce standardization of these names, a process in which many thousands of the old names were lost.

Surnames

Although up to the tenth century surnames in Ireland were not hereditary, the influence of the church, dating from this period, can still be seen in many common modern Irish surnames, in particular those beginning with 'Gil-' or 'Kil-', an anglicised version of the Irish Gi*olla*, meaning follower or devotee. Thus Gilmartin, in Irish *Mac Giolla Mhártain*, means 'son of a follower of (St) Martin'. Similarly, the church is the origin of all of those names starting with 'Mul-', a version of the Irish

Maol, meaning bald, and applied to the monks because of their distinctive tonsure. Thus Mulrennan (*Ó Maoilbhréanainn*) means 'descendant of a follower of St Brendan'.

While many of the names appearing in accounts of this time appear similar in form to modern Irish names, incorporating in particular the prefix 'mac' (meaning 'son of'), in fact they were not hereditary, lasting only

of the ancestor from whom descent is indicated. In many cases this ancestor can be quite accurately identified, and the origin of the name dated precisely. Thus, at the start of the eleventh century, Brian Boru possessed no surname, being simply 'Brian, High-King of the Irish', his grandson Teigue called himself *Ua Briain* in memory of his illustrious grandfather, and the name became hereditary thereafter. Similarly, the

The profusion of Irish surnames originating in the Church is a clear reflection of the depth of its early influence. The ruins of simple monastic settlements such as that at Kilree, Co. Kilkenny (left) are common and widespread. Even St Patrick's Cathedral in Dublin (facing page), now the national symbol of the Church of Ireland, stands on the site of a much simpler pre-Norman establishment.

one generation. Thus Turlough mac Airt, was Turlough, son of Art; his own son would be Conor mac Turlough, Conor son of Turlough.

Nonetheless, Ireland was one of the first European countries in which a system of fixed hereditary surnames developed. The earliest names appear to be those incorporating 'Ó' or its earlier form *Ua*, meaning 'grandson'. The first recorded fixed surname is O'Clery (*Ó Cléirigh*), as noted by the Annals, which record the death of Tigherneach Ua Cléirigh, Lord of Aidhne in Co. Galway in the year 916. It seems likely that this is the oldest surname recorded anywhere in Europe.

By the eleventh century many families had acquired true surnames as we would know them today. All of these surnames incorporate the same two basic elements, 'O' or 'Mac', together with the personal name

O'Neills derive their surname from Niall Glún Dubh, who died in 919.

Due to linguistic changes, the origins of many of the personal names such as Niall or Brian which form the stem of the surname remain obscure, but two broad categories can be distinguished: descriptive and occupational. In the first category, we can guess that the progenitor of the Traceys (*Ó Treasaigh*) was a formidable character, *treasach* meaning 'warlike', while the ancestor of the Duffs must have been dark-featured, since *dubh*, the root of the name, means black or dark. Among the occupations recorded in names are the churchmen dealt with above, clerks (Clery, *Ó Cléirigh*, from *cléireach*), bards (Ward, *Mac an Bháird*, from *bard*), spokesman (MacCloran, *Mac Labhráin*, from the Irish *labhraidh*), and smiths (McGowan, *Mac*

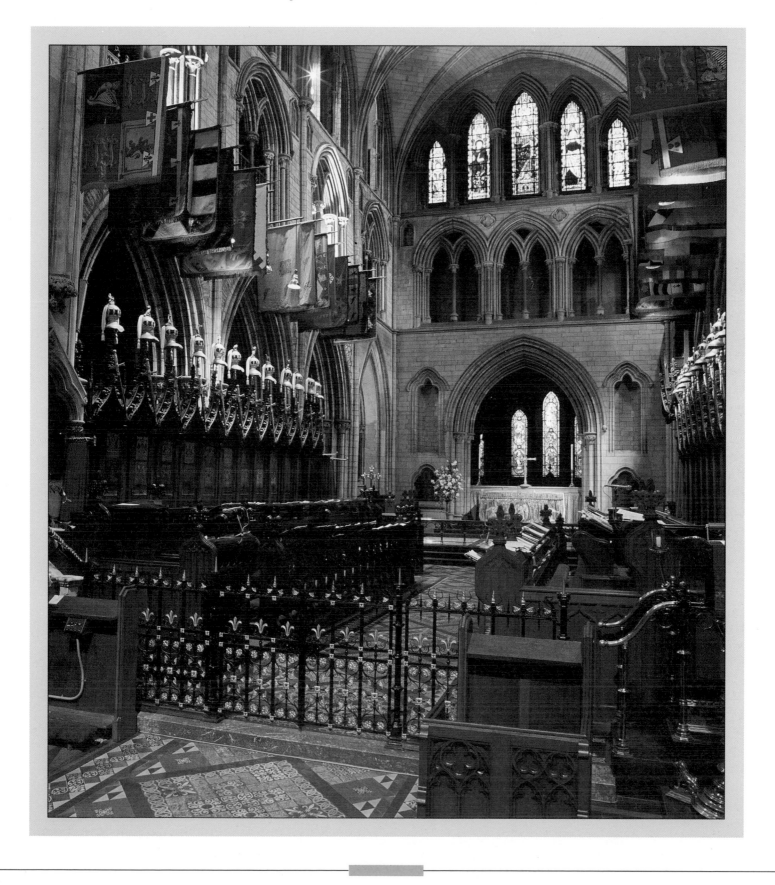

Gabhann, from *gabha*). One category of name, common in English, which is extremely rare among Irish names is the toponymic, deriving from the name of a locality. It seems likely that this reflects the fact that, for the Gaeil, who you were related to was much more important than where you came from.

Although the immediate reason for the early adoption of hereditary names in Ireland may have been a rapidly expanding population, it can also be seen as the logical outcome of a process at work from the times of the earliest tribal names. Originally, these indicated identification with a common god, often connected with an animal valued by the tribe, as in the case of the *Osrái*, or 'deer-people', for example. Next came identification with a divine ancestor, the *Bóinnrí*, for instance, claiming descent from the goddess Bóinn, the divinised river Boyne. Later the ancestor was merely legendary, as for the *Eoghanacht*, while later still the tribe claimed direct descent from a historical ancestor, as in the case of the *Uí Néill*. This slow emergence of kin-relationships out of religion and myth into the realm of history would seem to reach its logical conclusion with the adoption of hereditary surnames, permanent proof of verifiable ties of blood. On a more mundane level, of course, such proof was a valuable political asset, since it demonstrated membership of a powerful kin-group. Even today, the fact that all Gaelic names, with few exceptions, begin with O or Mac is undeniable and continuing proof of the significance of family and kin for the Irish.

Although it began early, the process of the creation of surnames was slow, and continued for over six hundred years. As the population grew and new families were formed, they sought to consolidate their identity by adopting hereditary surnames of their own, usually by simply adding *Mac* to the first name of the founding ancestor. In the course of this process, then, many surnames were created which are in fact offshoots of more common names. Thus, for example, the MacMahons and the McConsidines are descended from the O'Brien family, the former from Mahon O'Brien, who died in 1129, the latter from Constantine O'Brien, who died in 1193. The continuing division and sub-division of the most powerful Gaelic families like this is almost certainly the reason for the great proliferation of Gaelic surnames.

Physical features such as the Co. Waterford waterfall (top) and the Comeragh Mountains (right) are obvious and frequent sources of placenames, but ownership was often the most vivid distinguishing characteristic, as for MacGillycuddy's Reeks (above).

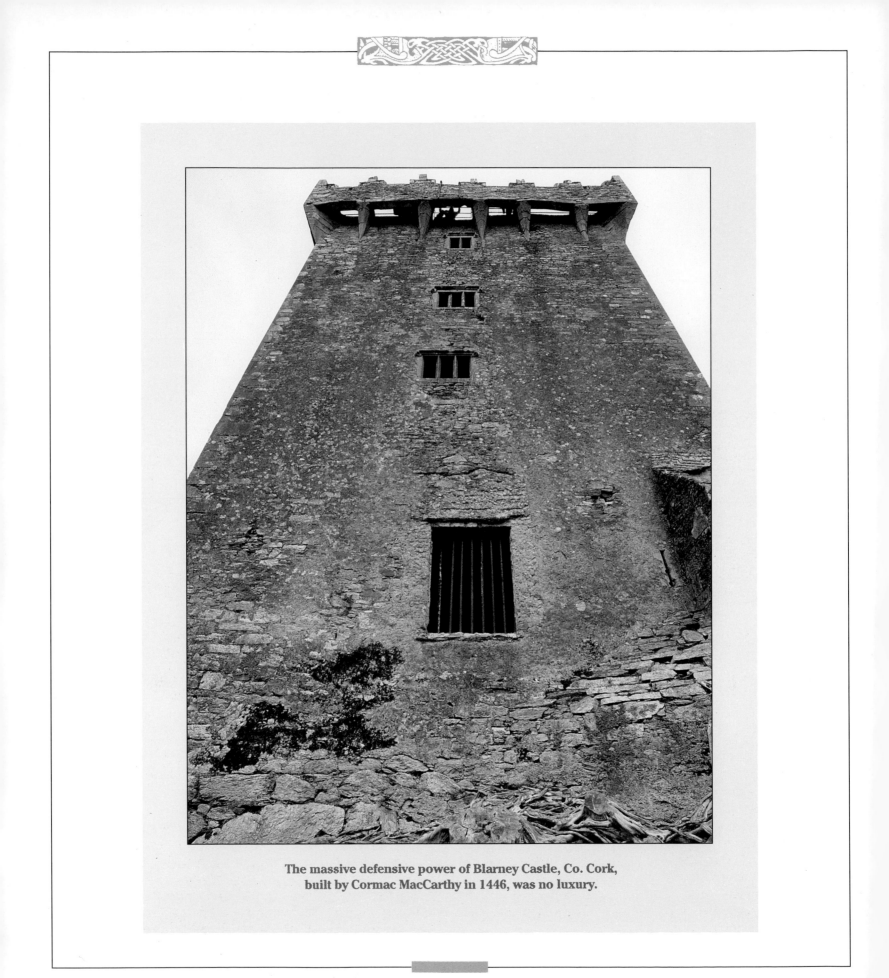

The massive defensive power of Blarney Castle, Co. Cork,
built by Cormac MacCarthy in 1446, was no luxury.

Clans and Families of Ireland

Invasion, Plantation and War

For at least 1,400 years, up to the ninth century, the civilization of Ireland remained uniformly Celtic. Then, in the year 795, came the first of the Viking attacks, on Lambay Island in Dublin Bay. This was the beginning of more than two centuries of attack and invasion which had a devastating effect on Ireland, and on the Irish monasteries in particular.

'Viking' (from the Old Norse *víkingr*) means 'sea-rover' or 'pirate', and this is precisely what these people were. Ethnically they were Teutons, Danish, Swedish and Norwegian farmers, fishermen and sea-merchants, who were forced onto the open sea in search of a

Round Castle, near the entrance to Bannow Harbour, Co. Kerry, part of the defences of the Earls of Desmond, who created what was in effect a separate state in south Munster.

livelihood by over-population and shortage of arable land. From the eighth century, their plundering raids terrorized much of the known world, reaching as far as America, North Africa, and Constantinople.

In Ireland, the annalists distinguished two groups among the raiding Vikings, the *Lochlannaigh*, or Norwegians, and the *Danair*, or Danes, the Norwegians

being described as fair, the Danish as dark. Initially the Norwegians dominated, and their raids were sporadic and unsystematic. From about 830, however, a new phase of large-scale attacks, involving the use of fleets of longships, began, and the Vikings penetrated deep inland through the use of rivers and lakes. Attracted by the wealth of the monasteries and churches, they plundered them steadily. From this period date the first of the Vikings' fortified settlements. In 852, the Danes wrested control of one of these settlements, the military and trading post of Dublin, from the Norwegians, under their king Olaf (in Irish *Amhlaoibh*), and founded the Danish kingdom of Dublin which was to last three hundred years, until the coming of the Anglo-Normans.

For the next 100 years, up to the middle of the tenth century, the Vikings consolidated and extended their power through unremitting aggression. From about 950 on, however, the east Clare Gaelic sept of the *Dál gCais* began its rise to power, capturing first the Kingship of Munster from the *Eoghanacht* and then, with Brian Boru, taking the high-kingship of Ireland from the *Uí Néill* in 1002. Brian fused the disparate Gaelic forces into a single confederate army, and defeated the combined might of the Norwegian and Danish forces in the battle of Clontarf on April 23, 1014, breaking the power of the Vikings permanently.

Although their political power declined rapidly after this, as a people the Vikings were soon thoroughly absorbed into the religious and political life of the country, adopting the Irish language and Irish customs, intermarrying and intermingling. Many modern Irish surnames reflect this, with McLoughlin (*Mac Lochlainn*) and McIvor (*Mac Íomhair*), for instance, deriving from a combination of the Gaelic patronymic with a Norse personal name. To them also we owe all of the earliest towns in the country: Dublin, Wexford, Waterford, Cork and Limerick all began as Viking settlements, and even after their absorption into the Gaelic culture the commercial interests of the newcomers kept them centred in these areas.

Ireland Before the Normans

For a century and a half after the battle of Clontarf the Irish provincial kings were locked in internecine warfare which proved just as devastating as the attacks of the Viking raiders. The man deposed by Brian Boru, Malachy II, resumed the high-kingship after Brian's death at Clontarf, but he was to be the last undisputed occupant of the throne. After this there were always at least two claimants at war with each other.

By now the large-scale divisions of the country had evolved considerably, although the earlier tribal territories were still the basis of political geography. There were five major areas: Leinster, Meath, Munster, Ulster and Connacht. Leinster, covering most of the traditional territory of the *Laighin*, was ruled by the MacMurrough family, based at Ferns in Co. Wexford. Meath was still the preserve of the southern *Uí Néill*, of whom Malachy II was the last to aspire to the high kingship. In Connacht, the ruling family was the O'Connors, although a number of powerful sub-kingdoms existed, in which their authority remained weak. One such sub-kingdom was *Breifne*, covering parts of the modern counties of Sligo, Leitrim, Cavan and Monaghan, and ruled by the O'Rourkes. Munster was chiefly under the power of the O'Brien family, the dynasty founded by Brian Boru, but their supremacy was continually challenged by the powerful *Eoghanacht* family of the MacCarthys. In Ulster, four individual kingdoms existed, Tirconnell, Tirowen, Uriel and Ulaidh, ruled, respectively, by the O'Donnells (part of the northern *Uí Néill*), the MacLochlainns, the O'Carrolls, and the MacDonlevys.

The Normans

The Normans were descendants of Vikings who, by the early tenth century, had established themselves firmly in a large area around the lower Seine in France, later known as Normandy, and, like the Vikings in Ireland, had been assimilated into French society. They soon acquired a reputation for military sophistication, and were active in many of the European wars. In 1066, with only 5,000 men, William, Duke of Normandy, took the crown of England, and over the next century the Normans set up a strong kingdom in England, and solidly established themselves in Scotland and Wales.

It was the incessant warfare among the provincial kings, and the resulting shifts in power and allegiance, which ultimately led to the arrival of the Normans in

Round towers (facing page) were a desperate defensive response by the Irish monasteries to the growing threat of Viking invaders. Their effectiveness in providing refuge during raids seems doubtful.

Above: the marriage of Aoife, daughter of Dermot MacMurrough, to Strongbow, depicted by Daniel Maclise as the symbolic source of Ireland's subsequent catastrophes. Right: the Norman castle at Trim, built in the thirteenth century by the de Lacys, is one of the largest in Ireland.

Ireland. In 1166 Mac Lochlainn, king of Tirowen and claimant of the high-kingship, was killed in a rebellion of the northern sub-kings and the O'Connors of Connacht. As a result, his ally Dermot MacMurrough, king of Leinster, was expelled from his kingdom, and went to seek help across the Irish sea. When he had outlined to Henry II and his barons the profits to be made from involvement in Ireland, they lost little time in organizing a succession of expeditions. The first of these, under Robert Fitzstephen, landed at Bannow Bay in Wexford on May 1, 1169. It was quickly followed by others, and with the help of MacMurrough's men the Normans took Wexford town and launched successful attacks north and east into Offaly and Ossory. The Irish, under the

new high-king Rory O'Connor, put up stiff resistance, however, and it was not until the arrival of Strongbow, Richard Fitzgilbert de Clare, in August 1170, that the Norman invasion was assured of success. By the autumn of 1171 Strongbow was master of Dublin, Wexford and Waterford, and was launching attacks into *Breifne* and Meath.

In October 1171 Henry II himself arrived to secure his own power, over both the Norman invaders and the Irish kings, and quickly achieved both objectives. Many

their methods of government to suit Irish conditions – accepting, for example, the provincial divisions – in those areas where they had greatest control they soon began to superimpose the political divisions which had existed in England since the Anglo-Saxons: the shires. By the early fourteenth century there were twelve of these: Dublin, Carlow, Louth, Roscommon, Cork, Kerry, Tipperary, Limerick, Kildare, Waterford, Meath and Connacht, all but the last in more or less the form they are known today.

Above: the seal and (right) the tomb of Strongbow, displaying the Normans' pride in their military prowess.

of the Irish, including O'Brien, MacCarthy and O'Rourke, submitted to him, and Strongbow's power was curbed by confining him to Leinster, with Dublin, Wexford and Waterford removed from his jurisdiction.

From now on, the process for the Normans was one of consolidation and expansion. Castle-building was one of the fundamental elements of their practice; as they took control of an area, a fortress, initially in wood, later in stone, was erected to help retain that control. Around the castles, churches and other buildings were built, and from these grew many of the present towns of Ireland, for example Athlone, Carrickfergus, and Nenagh. It was the Normans, too, who began the creation of what are now the counties of Ireland. Although they adapted

Over the next 300 years, the history of Ireland is a kaleidoscope of Gaelic and Norman advance and retreat. Until the thirteenth century Norman progress was steady, encroaching on the old Gaelic families, displacing and subduing them. From the second half of the thirteenth century, however, the native lords began a resistance struggle which had Leinster, Connacht and Meath in virtual continual revolt, and which culminated in the invasion of Edward Bruce, invited from Scotland in 1314 by the Gaelic lords. The invasion failed, but demonstrated graphically the tenuousness of Norman control over many areas of the country.

Theoretically, Ireland was governed by English law, and subject to a royal administration centred in Dublin.

In fact, effective royal jurisdiction was confined to the Pale, an area centred around Dublin which grew and shrank with the fortunes of the English in Ireland; by 1537, with the resurgence of native influence, the Pale included only Dublin and some parts of counties Meath, Louth and Kildare.

Outside the Pale, many of the Norman lords governed their lands independently of English law; the Fitzgeralds, Earls of Desmond, rulers of most of counties Kerry, Limerick, Cork and Waterford, operated what was in effect an independent state in the southern part of the country through most of the fifteenth and sixteenth centuries. Apart from the great Norman lords – Burke and Bermingham in Connacht, Fitzgerald, Fitzmaurice and Barry in Munster, the Butlers in Kilkenny – many of the original Gaelic families retained and extended effective control over their traditional lands, while others,

Above and above left: Blarney Castle. The MacCarthys retained possession of their lands into the seventeenth century, due in part to such Norman-style defences.

displaced by the Normans, moved to neighbouring areas and drove out the original inhabitants. It was in Ulster that the Normans made least headway; the O'Neills and O'Donnells in particular had successfully resisted their expansion, and continually pushed back the borders of the Norman lands.

Ultimately more successful than military pressure was the attraction exerted by Gaelic society. Slowly over the centuries, the Norman families outside the Pale intermarried with the Irish and adopted their language and customs, until by the sixteenth century they had more in common with the native Irish than with England, in whose name they held power.

The extent of the intermingling of Norman and Gaelic is illustrated graphically in the history of surnames of Norman origin. These are numerous and widespread throughout the country, and most of them were created in the aftermath of the Norman invasion; names such as Browne, Burke, Cusack, Keating, Power, Walsh. Whatever their current form, virtually all of these originated in Norman-French, either linked to a particular placename in Normandy or Wales, or as a French descriptive. Thus *de Burgo* or *de Burgh*, the original version of Burke, comes from Tonburg in Normandy, while *le Poer*, the original for Power, comes from *le povre*, meaning 'the poor one'. The names now most obviously of Norman origin are those beginning with 'Fitz', a corruption of the French *fils*, meaning 'son', and used by the Normans in the same way as the Gaels used *Mac*. Of course, as well as those of purely Norman origin, the twelfth-century invaders also included many of Breton and Flemish extraction. Irish names of Breton origin include Dillon (*de Leon*, from Leon in Brittany) and Brett (*le Breton*), while Flemish examples

Art MacMurrough Kavanagh attacking the Earl of Gloucester, from a contemporary French miniature. The military mismatch between the barefoot Irish and the armour-clad Anglo-Normans is typical, as is the Irish attack emerging from forest and mountain.

include Fleming, Roche (*de la Roche*) and Wall (*de Vale*).

As the Normans were assimilated into Gaelic culture their surnames underwent the same process of subdivision already seen in Gaelic surnames. Thus, for example, in the thirteenth century the descendants of Piers de Birmingham were calling themselves *Mac Fheorais,* Irish for 'son of Piers', which was later anglicised as 'Corish'. In the same way, Jocelyn (in Irish *Goisdelbh*) de Angulo was the ancestor of the family of *MacGoisdealbhaigh*, anglicised Costello, while the fragmentation of the powerful *de Burgo* (Burke) family of Connacht led to such surname offshoots as MacWalter, MacSheoinín (later anglicised as 'Jennings'), MacMyler and MacDavid.

THE TERRITORIES OF THE GREAT FAMILIES OF IRELAND IN THE FOURTEENTH CENTURY

O'Doherty

MacSweeney

MacDonnell

MacSweeney

O'Cahan

O'DONNELL

O'NEILL

Maguire

O'Neill
Clanaboy

Earldom
of
Ulster

Barrett

O'Dowd

O'Rourke

O'Connor

O'Hara

O'Gara

MacDonagh

MacMahon

McGuinness

O'Malley

MacDermot

O'Farrell

O'Reilly

Plunket

Costello

O'Connor
Don

Preston

O'Flaherty

O'Kelly

Bermingham

Barnewall

Blake

O'Madden

Burke

St. Laurence

O'Carroll

O'Connor

Earldom
of
Kildare

O'Molloy

O'Dunn

O'Brien

O'More

O'Toole

MacNamara

O'Kennedy

Fitzgerald

O'Byrne

Burke

Butler
of
Ormond

MacMurrogh

Fitzmaurice

Fitzgerald

Roche

Earldom
of
Desmond

MacCarthy Mor

Power

O'Sullivan

Fitzgerald

O'Sullivan

Barry

MacCarthy

O'Driscoll

Tudor Plantations

Throughout the fifteenth and early sixteenth centuries, the rulers of England were too preoccupied elsewhere to devote energy and resources to Ireland, and the absorption of the Norman newcomers reflected the weakness of English power. With the accession of Henry VIII, this changed. Henry set out to turn the fiction of English rule into fact, by demanding recognition of his authority from the semi-independent Gaelic and Norman lords in return for his granting them legal title to their lands. Under this arrangement, forty of the most powerful lords accepted his authority, some of them receiving English titles also: O'Brien became Earl of Thomond, O'Neill Earl of Tyrone, Burke of Galway Earl of Clanrickard. As well as ruling indirectly through them, Henry also extended direct royal rule throughout Leinster and into parts of Munster. In the areas controlled directly by the crown strenuous efforts were made to introduce the Reformation, dissolving the monasteries and attempting to introduce doctrinal reforms. In this, neither he nor following English rulers had much success, either with the Gaelic population or with the Old English, as the descendants of the Normans were now known. From this period, the conflicts between English and Irish were sharpened by differences of religion.

Henry's daughter, Mary, began the process of plantation which was to change the social composition of the country permanently. Under this process, land held by the native or Old English lords was declared forfeit to the crown, for a variety of possible reasons, the most usual being disloyalty or rebellion. The land was then granted to English settlers, who were expected to anglicise the area. The first plantations were carried out in 1556, in counties Laois and Offaly, renamed Queen's and King's counties, and were fiercely resisted, as a result achieving only partial success. Plantation policy was continued under Elizabeth, with the largest covering the forfeited lands of the Earls of Desmond in Munster in 1586.

All of these plantations were severely disrupted by the great rebellion which broke out in 1594. Up to this period, Ulster had been least affected by the steady encroachments of the English on the native lands, and the Gaelic Ulster lords had maintained almost total independence over the centuries. Now, however, they recognized the danger to their own power, and by 1595 Hugh O'Neill, Hugh O'Donnell and Hugh Maguire were waging open war against the English. In response, Elizabeth committed massive numbers of troops, and her best generals, and the Irish were finally defeated at the battle of Kinsale in 1601. This defeat marked the end of the Gaelic lordship, and the start of the final collapse of Gaelic society.

The Ulster Plantation

In Ulster, the defeat of the Gaelic aristocracy and the subsequent escape to the continent of almost 100 of the most important leaders, left a vacuum, which Elizabeth's successor, James I, was quick to fill. In 1609 the Plantation of Ulster was declared, affecting the entire counties of Armagh, Tyrone, Fermanagh, Donegal, Cavan and Coleraine (now Derry or Londonderry). Of the estimated 3,800,000 acres involved, 1,500,000, partly or wholly infertile, were set aside for the native Irish. Over one-and-a-half million acres of the remainder was given in grants to schools, the Church of Ireland, the military, and institutions; for instance, in exchange for financial backing the entire county of Coleraine was granted to the guilds of the city of London, and renamed Londonderry. The rest of the land was set aside for colonization, with large estates granted at nominal rents on condition that the landlord let the land only to English or Scots tenants.

Unlike the earlier plantations further south, the plantation of Ulster was highly successful. Although it did not fully achieve its aim of clearing certain areas completely of the native Irish – despite the terms of the land grants many of them managed to remain as tenants – it nonetheless attracted a massive influx of settlers. A very large proportion of these were Scots Calvinists, drawn by the relative freedom from religious intolerance in what was seen very much as frontier territory, and their names, Ross, Kerr, Graham, Morrison, Stewart, still predominate throughout many areas of Ulster today.

The situation in the two northeastern counties of Ulster, Antrim and Down, was different. Connections of trade and blood had existed between Scotland and the coastal areas of these counties for centuries, and the highly successful private plantations undertaken in the counties by Sir Arthur Chichester, Hugh Montgomery, and James Hamilton from 1605 simply accelerated a process already under way.

Above: Oliver Cromwell, the Lord Protector. His name is still reviled in Ireland, both for the ruthless slaughter he inflicted and for the massive dispossessions that followed his victory. The policies of Elizabeth I (facing page) were less genocidal, but played an equally large part in bringing about the final collapse of the old order.

Apart from Ulster, the early seventeenth century also saw plantations carried out in Leitrim, Longford, King's County, Queen's County, Westmeath and Longford. These were much less thorough than those in the north, however, retaining native tenants and placenames, and achieved only limited success. In general, the settlers in these areas were English, known as the New English to distinguish them from the Catholic descendants of the Normans, the Old English.

The Wars of the Seventeenth Century

The dispossessions of Gaelic and Old English families by the plantations, and the introduction of a new colonial population into Ulster, produced enormous discontent;

by the 1640s the country was ripe for rebellion. In October 1641 a rising of the native Irish began, led from the north by Sir Felim O'Neill, Rory O'More and Lord Maguire. In the fierce and bloody fighting which followed, the rebels took control of almost the whole province of Ulster, along with parts of Leinster. After a delay of two months the rebels were joined by the Old English and, by February 1642, the entire country, with the exception of parts of Cork, Donegal and Antrim, was in rebel hands. At this point the English Parliament passed the 'Adventurers' Act', promising the repayment in Irish land of money advanced by individuals to help suppress the Irish rebellion. This was the start of a process of land transfer and colonization much more extensive than anything attempted up to now.

Throughout the 1640s the Confederation of Old English and Irish, though divided among themselves, fought a bitter war, first against the crown, then against the winning side in the English Civil War, the parliamentary forces. By the time Cromwell arrived in Ireland in 1649 the Confederate forces were weak, and the efficient ferocity of Cromwell's campaign, with massacres at Drogheda, Wexford and elsewhere, broke the rebellion. With the final surrender of Galway in May 1652, the entire country was subdued. The final price of the decade of war was high, with famine, abject poverty and disease rampant throughout the country.

After the end of the civil war there was immense pressure on the English government to settle debts, both to the 'adventurers' who had financed the war and to the soldiers who had fought in it; Irish land was to be the principal currency used. A massive programme of confiscations began, aimed at transplanting all Irish landowners to Connacht and Clare, and distributing their land to the government's creditors. In all, 11,000,000 acres of land were seized, to be divided among 1,000 adventurers and 35,000 soldiers. Although in some ways successful, effecting a huge transfer of land ownership in a very short time, the results were not always as intended. The main class affected by transplantation was that of uninfluential landowners; those at the very top of the scale, the great magnates, and those at the bottom, the tenants and landless, remained where they were, while many of the adventurers and soldiers to whom land was given simply sold out as soon as possible; less than a quarter of them eventually settled in Ireland.

Despite the disasters of the first half of the seventeenth century, many of the native Irish still cherished hopes of regaining their ancestral lands, and the restoration of the Stuart kings of England provided a natural focus for these hopes. Faced with the threat of a fast-expanding Protestant population, swelled during the 1650s by the continuing influx of Scots Presbyterians and the arrival of the Quakers, Baptists and Congregationalists, the Catholics enthusiastically welcomed the accession of James II to the English throne in 1685 and embraced his policy of Catholicization with relish; by the end of 1688 Catholics were dominant in the army, the judiciary, the administration and the town corporations. When James lost his throne to his Protestant son-in-law, William of Orange, Ireland was the natural base from which to attempt to regain it.

By the time he arrived in Ireland in March 1689, only Enniskillen and Londonderry remained under Protestant control. Despite a massive siege mounted against it by James, Londonderry managed to hold out, a victory which proved to be of great significance in the campaign. After this, James remained somewhat inactive until William arrived at Carrickfergus in June 1690. The decisive confrontation between the two armies took place at the Boyne in July 1690, where William triumphed. The Jacobite armies retreated west across the country, and James himself fled to France. The war continued for another fifteen months, until October 1691, when it was formally ended by the Treaty of Limerick.

One of the most important provisions of this treaty was to permit Jacobite officers and men to go into exile. More than 11,000 sailed to France, where they joined the French army and formed the famous Irish Brigade. This, the 'Flight of the Wild Geese', was the start of a long tradition of Irish service in the Continental armies, with more than half a million Irishmen joining the French army alone between 1691 and 1791. From these men descend many renowned French families, such as MacMahon, Lally, O'Farrell and O'Kelly.

The end of the Williamite War marked the final success of English rule in Ireland, and began a period in which the new settlers of the seventeenth century could begin to feel themselves secure in their possessions, and at home in their new country. Over the course of the century, a huge transfer in land ownership had been imposed – in 1603, 90 per cent of Irish land had been in the hands of Catholics, while by 1691 they owned less than 14 per cent. In the process a massive influx of English and Scots had taken place which, in the case of Ulster in particular, radically altered the composition of society.

The old Gaelic world was never to recover from the final collapse of the seventeenth century. Although vestiges of the old culture survived underground in poetry, music and folklore, English ways were now dominant, and this extended even to the old surnames. From about this time, the prefixes O and Mac began to be dropped, and the names themselves were anglicised and distorted. English officials and landlords, unfamiliar with Irish, transliterated, translated, and mistranslated. Thus, for example, *Ó hArrachtáin*, common in Cork and Kerry, was changed to Harrington, its nearest-sounding English equivalent. Other names were translated, *Mac Gabhann* (son of the smith) becoming Smith in some areas, while remaining McGowan in others, and *Mac Giolla Easpaig* (son of the follower of the bishop) becoming either Gillespie or, simply, Bishop. A large number of ludicrous mistranslations also date from this time. To take one example only: *Mac an Déaghanaigh* (son of the dean) became Bird in many places, because of a spurious phonetic resemblance to the Irish for bird, *éan*. Previous Gaelic attitudes to such names underline the sharp ironies of this process. When the influx of settlers began in the seventeenth century, the Gaelic poets ridiculed the new surnames; in Irish society, the function of the surname, with O or Mac, was to indicate kinship, and such names as White, Black, Bird or Smith were simply absurd and laughable. Within less than a century, the names they had mocked were being forced on them.

William of Orange, whose victories in Ireland signalled the
end of any hope for the restoration of the old Gaelic order.

Newcomers and Emigrants

Around the start of the eighteenth century, as Irish conditions became more settled, two groups of Continental Protestant refugees were settled in the country with official or semi-official help. The first of these, the Huguenots, were French Calvinists persecuted intermittently by the Catholic rulers of France throughout the seventeenth century. Small numbers of refugees from this persecution had come to Ireland, mainly via England, from 1620 to 1641, and again with Cromwell in 1649, but it was in 1685, after the revocation of the Edict of Nantes, which had guaranteed them toleration, that the main body of Huguenots began to

The Irish House of Commons, though rigidly confined to the Anglo-Irish, became the focus for a growing sense of independence and Irish identity in the eighteenth century.

arrive, mostly from the countryside around the city of La Rochelle in the modern region of Poitou-Charente. After the end of the Williamite wars, large Huguenot settlements were established in Portarlington, Youghal, Cork, Dublin, Waterford and Lisburn, where they became celebrated for their expertise in textiles, specialising in weaving, lace-making, and glove-making. In the course

Jonathan Swift, son of an English immigrant to Ireland, and confidant of English prime ministers, exhorted his Irish readers to "burn everything English but their coal".

of time, they became thoroughly absorbed into Irish society through intermarriage, and names such as Boucicault, Maturin, Le Fanu and Trench are still familiar in Ireland today.

The Palatines

The second wave of Protestant refugees were the Palatine Germans. In early May 1709, thousands of the inhabitants of the countryside of Hesse and Baden, near the city of Mannheim, were forced off their land by the wars between Louis XIV and a confederacy that included England. They made their way to Rotterdam, and from there to London in English ships. The English appear to have been ill-prepared to receive them, and over 800 families, more than 6,000 people, were despatched to Ireland between September 1709 and January 1710.

Initially there was some difficulty in placing the Palatines; of 538 families first taken on as tenants by Anglo-Irish landlords, 352 were reported to have deserted their holdings, and a good number of these returned to England. However, some of the settlements were highly successful, in particular that on the Southwell lands around Rathkeale in Co. Limerick in 1712. One hundred and fifty families settled here on very favourable terms, and within a few years were fully engaged in the production of hemp, flax and cattle. A second successful and sizeable settlement of Palatine families was carried out on the lands of Abel Ram, near Gorey in Co. Wexford around the same period. The distinctive Palatine way of life endured in these areas until well into the nineteenth century. Evidence of their eventual full absorption into the life of the country is found today in the geographical spread of the distinctive surnames of their descendants: Switzer, Ruttle, Sparling, Tesky and Fitzell.

The Anglo-Irish

Along with these readily-identifiable immigrant groups, the eighteenth century also saw the rise of a much more powerful, though less well defined race, the Anglo-Irish. These were a social elite, dominating politics, the law, land, and the professions, who were descended from Norman, Old English, Cromwellian or even, in some rare cases, Old Gaelic stock. Rather than a common ethnic origin, what defined this people was their own sense of belonging, derived from a confused colonial nationalism. This is reflected in their use of the word 'Irish'. Those who, in 1690, were 'the Protestants of Ireland' or 'the English of this Kingdom', by the 1720s could call themselves, simply, 'Irish gentlemen'; whereas previously 'Irish' had meant 'native Irish', it was now extended to cover those who had been outsiders. There remained, however, a fatal ambiguity in its use. The continuing threat posed to the position of the Anglo-Irish by the overwhelming majority of the population – Gaelic, Catholic, and living in a degree of poverty that astounded foreign observers – meant that they simply could not afford to identify too closely with the country as a whole. As a result, in the writings of the time 'the Irish', or even 'the Irish race' most often refers specifically to the people we now call Anglo-Irish.

The best-known representative of the Anglo-Irish was Dr Jonathan Swift, poet, satirist, and Dean of St Patrick's Cathedral, Dublin, and the dilemma of his race is illustrated vividly in his work. Fighting bitterly against the poverty and injustice which he saw inflicted on

The design for the funeral of the Countess of Ormond in 1601, as recorded by a contemporary heraldic artist. The love of elaborate ceremonial was always a feature of the Anglo-Irish Establishment.

Ireland by the self-interest of the English government, his struggle was nonetheless largely on behalf of his fellow Irish Protestants. At the same time, he was aware that such formulations of his as 'government without the consent of the governed is the very definition of slavery' could apply just as well to the relationship between Anglo-Irish and Gaelic Irish as it could to the relationship between the English government and the Anglo-Irish. In attacking injustice done to his own race, he was in the peculiar and uncomfortable position of implicitly attacking injustice done by them. In Swift's case at least, common humanity could outweigh partisan considerations, and some of his most famous work is universal in its implications. *A Modest Proposal*, for instance, in response to mass starvation among the most destitute Irish, satirically suggests selling their young children as food for gentlemen, even offering some helpful recipes.

Although real power emanated from London, within Ireland the Anglo-Irish were dominant for over two centuries, and much of the character of the country today derives from their influence. They were responsible for the great neo-classical houses of the gentry, the Georgian buildings and thoroughfares of Dublin, and the literary tradition which lay behind the great revival of writing in Ireland in the early twentieth century.

49

The Penal Laws

In homogenizing the mixed origins of the Anglo-Irish, the one decisive factor was Anglicanism; membership of the Church of Ireland was an absolute prerequisite for advancement or power. The key mechanism for the retention and reinforcement of this power was provided by a whole series of measures, known collectively as the Penal Laws. In theory, these placed fanatically detailed restrictions on the property rights, social rights and religious practice of non-Anglicans, denying them, for example, the right to take leases or own land above a certain value, outlawing Catholic clergy, forbidding higher education and entry to the professions, and imposing oaths of conformity to the state church, the Church of Ireland. Thorough enforcement of many of these laws was never a practical proposition, given the make-up of the population, but they nonetheless had a profound effect. To take one area only, by the time the laws began to be relaxed somewhat in the 1770s, only five per cent of the land of the country remained in Catholic hands.

Ulster Emigration

Although more than a quarter of the population of Ireland in the eighteenth century was Protestant, the Anglo-Irish Anglicans made up only a minority of this. It was the Ulster settlers and their descendants, overwhelmingly Presbyterian, who were in the the majority. The Penal Laws, designed as they were to protect the privileges of members of the Church of Ireland, disenfranchised and discriminated against Presbyterians as well as Catholics, though the effects were mitigated to some extent by their superior economic strength and the tight-knit communities in which they lived. Nonetheless, to a people who had originally fled Scotland to escape religious persecution, the impositions of the Penal Laws were intolerable. This was reflected in the increasing radicalization of Ulster opinion, which was to reach its peak in the rebellion of 1798, but also in emigration from Ulster to America. This was the start of a process with far-reaching consequences. Up to now, the movement of peoples had been into Ireland. Now began the long exodus.

As well as political discontent, this first movement of emigration also had economic causes. The large majority of Ulster Presbyterians were poor smallholders,

artisans, weavers and labourers, all most vulnerable both to the succession of natural disasters – crop failures, smallpox epidemics, livestock diseases – which recurred throughout the eighteenth century, and to the increasing commercialization of Ulster, with the constant efforts of landlords to increase the profitability of their lands by raising rents. The increasing importance of the linen trade was also influential, and the numbers of emigrants grew and fell as this trade prospered or faltered. The very nature of the business facilitated emigration, since the ships which brought flax seed from America often returned with a cargo of emigrants. Before 1720 the stream of migrants across the Atlantic was slow but steady, with New England the favoured

Above: the wild splendour of the Wicklow Mountains framed by the elegant terracing of Powerscourt Demesne. For the Anglo-Irish, part of the charm of such careful landscaping would have come from its reflection of the political relationship between themselves and the Gaelic Irish. Trinity College, Dublin (left) was at the very heart of the Anglo-Irish Establishment.

destination. After that date, the rate of emigration grew, with a peak in the late 1720s, and a decline in the 1730s, when relative prosperity returned to Ulster. The famine of 1740-41 gave a sharp impetus to the renewal of emigration, which rose steadily through the 1760s, when over 20,000 people left from the Ulster ports of Newry,

Portrush, Belfast, Larne and Londonderry. The migration reached a climax in the years 1770-74, when at least 30,000 people departed. Over the course of the whole century, it is estimated that more than 400,000 emigrated from Ulster, the vast majority to North America; in 1790, the United States' population of Irish stock has been estimated at 447,000, two-thirds of them originating from Ulster.

Those who left were mostly indentured labourers, contracting to work for a number of years for employers in Colonial America in return for their passage, and included very few convicts or independent travellers. One important result, and a significant difference with later, Catholic, emigration, is the fact that the move was often effected by entire families or even communities, allowing the settlers to maintain their way of life in the New World, and providing a continuity of religion and

Charles Carroll (above left), whose grandfather left Ireland for America in 1688, was the only Catholic signatory of the Declaration of Independence. Presidents Andrew Jackson (top) and Woodrow Wilson (above) are among the most prominent of the descendants of the eighteenth-century Scots-Irish emigrants.

tradition in keeping with the religious and cultural separateness they had already brought with them from Scotland to Ireland. To point up this separateness, in America they called themselves 'Scots-Irish', and the distinctive culture they maintained allows us to trace their settlements in the United States with some precision. Initially, most of the emigrants sailed to the Delaware estuary, especially to Pennsylvania, where Cumberland County became the effective centre of the

Scots-Irish settlement. In the 1730s, a second wave of emigrants, accompanied by the children of earlier settlers, moved further west in Pennsylvania and south into the Valley of Virginia. By the 1750s a third movement pushed further south again into the Carolina and Georgia back-country, where they met and mixed with emigrants arriving through southern seaports such as Charleston and Savannah. By the 1790s more than half the settlers along the Appalachian frontier were of Ulster lineage. The influence of their culture, their music, religion and way of life, can still be seen in these areas today.

The blend of Protestant evangelism, fierce self-sufficiency and political radicalism which many Ulster Presbyterians brought with them to the New World was powerfully influential in the American Revolution. In all the states, but especially in Pennsylvania, New Jersey, New York, Delaware and Maryland, the immigrant Scots-Irish and their descendants played a role in the war out of all proportion to their numbers; as an officer on the British side put it, 'call this war by whatever name you may, only call it not an American rebellion; it is nothing more or less than a Scotch Irish Presbyterian rebellion'. After American independence, the Scots-Irish tradition continued to play an important part in American life; the great nineteenth-century steel-producing town of Pittsburgh was created by Scots-Irish entrepreneurs, and their representatives are found at all levels of American society, in the professions, industry, finance, education, and with presidents such as Andrew Jackson and Woodrow Wilson.

1798

Ulster radicalism also found another outlet at home. Throughout the eighteenth century, local secret societies, such as the 'Hearts of Steel' and the 'Hearts of Oak', had sprung up, dedicated to defending their members, generally the poorest tenants. This tradition, along with the influence of the French and American Revolutions, provided the background for the United Irishmen, an organization dedicated to republican ideals and incorporating Catholic, Presbyterian and Anglo-Irish radicals. On May 23rd 1798, a rebellion against British rule organized by the United Irishmen broke out, with risings in Meath, Carlow, Kildare, Wicklow, Dublin and Wexford in the east, Antrim and Down in Ulster, and, with the assistance of a French invasion, in Mayo in the west. Over the course of the next six months the

Mathew Carey was forced to flee Ireland in 1784 for criticising the British government in print. He continued his radical journalism in the United States.

rebellion was crushed by the British, at great cost to lives and property; over 30,000 people died, and a million pounds worth of property was destroyed. Although the ideals of fraternity and religious equality which inspired the United Irishmen were defeated, many of the post-1798 refugees to the United States took those ideals with them, and many of them rose to social and political prominence. Another result of the failure of 1798 was an increase in pressure for Union between Ireland and Britain. The subsequent abolition of the Irish parliament and Irish self-government was one of the reasons for the huge increase in emigration from Ireland in the nineteenth century.

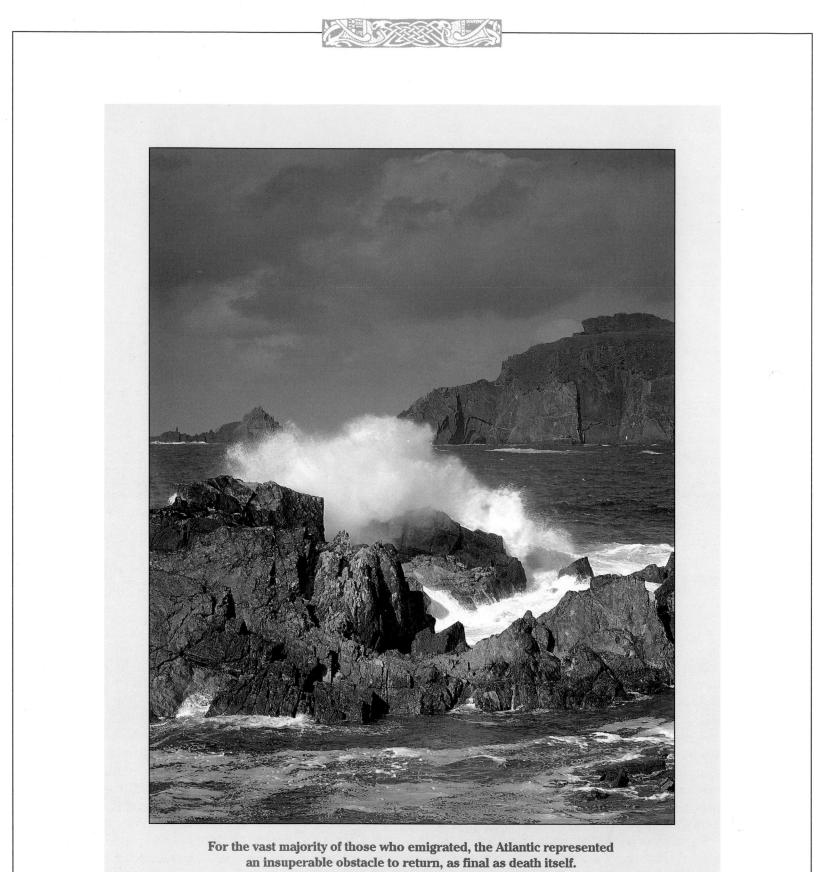

For the vast majority of those who emigrated, the Atlantic represented
an insuperable obstacle to return, as final as death itself.

Clans and Families of Ireland

Emigration and the Famine

The rock-strewn landscape of the Curraghmore Valley, Co. Kerry.

The traditional view of emigration in Presbyterian Ulster differed greatly from the image prevalent among the great mass of the population: the Gaelic Catholics. Whereas, in the popular mythology of the Scots-Irish, the New World offered an almost biblical deliverance from religious intolerance and economic oppression, for the Catholics emigration meant exile, in the phrase used by the Irish monastic missionaries of the early middle ages, a 'white martyrdom', second in suffering only to death itself. Allied to this overwhelmingly negative view of emigration, related, no doubt, to the traditional importance of extended kin-relationships in Gaelic life and strengthened by the enforced departure of the Gaelic aristocracy in the seventeenth century, were the practical barriers. Until 1780, Catholic immigration was officially forbidden in the Americas, and even if they possessed the inclination and the ingenuity to get to America, few of the Catholic Irish had the means. Nonetheless, some Catholic emigration did take place. As a result of the trade between the American

Victorian workhouses in Ireland were deliberately harsh and inhumane, to prevent 'abuse' by the lazy. By the middle of the nineteenth century mass desperation had swamped the system.

colonies and such southern ports as Cork and Kinsale, some Catholic Irish did manage to settle in the new colonies, particularly in Virginia and Maryland, where such names as 'New Ireland' and 'New Munster' appear. The most substantial Irish connection at this period, however, was with the West Indies. In the seventeenth century, in the aftermath of the Cromwellian wars, substantial numbers of the most destitute were shipped as slaves to 'the Barbadoes', and relatively large numbers of voluntary emigrants are also recorded in Jamaica, the Leeward Islands, and Montserrat, as well as in Barbados. As the slave-based economy of these areas grew, however, opportunities for poor white settlers diminished, and during the 1700s most of the Irish Catholics moved from the West Indies to the mainland

colonies. Another route for emigrants at this period was to Newfoundland, which maintained strong ties with Waterford and Wexford. In 1776, three to five thousand were reported to be leaving annually from these areas on Newfoundland ships, and by 1784 seven-eighths of the population of St John's, Newfoundland, was Irish-born.

When compared with the exodus from Ulster, however, Catholic emigration before the nineteenth century was relatively insignificant. Even after 1780, when the new egalitarian republic of the United States might have been expected to attract large numbers, migration remained very low. In part, this was due to new practical problems: the series of wars lasting right up to the final defeat of Napoleon in 1814 severely disrupted shipping, and made the journey across the Atlantic dangerous and difficult. There is no doubt, though, that relative prosperity at home, combined with the continuing view of emigration as a last resort, were the principal brakes on potential emigration.

Australia

The negative popular vision of emigration can only have been reinforced by the start of transportation of Irish convicts to Australia in 1780. The offences for which transportation could be imposed were manifold, ranging from the pettiest of thefts to 'treasonous' political crimes; by 1803, of the 2,086 Irish convicts in Australia, 40 per cent were political prisoners and the remainder sentenced for criminal offences. By 1836 there were about 20,000 Irish in the country and in 1861, three years after transportation had ended, the Irish community constituted almost 20 per cent of the population of Australia. Because of the distance involved, the journey was very costly, and this meant that very few arrived without assistance of some sort, either the unwelcome assistance of transportation, or one of the many schemes, in general privately funded, which evolved over the course of the nineteenth century. These schemes to subsidize the cost of the journey were aimed specifically at encouraging the migration of family groups and those with skills, and resulted in many communities leaving en masse; once a network of family ties existed in Australia into which new emigrants could fit, the breaking of the links with Ireland became easier. In the late nineteenth century, during the New Zealand gold rush, the numbers of Irish entering that country grew dramatically, and a strong Irish settlement developed along the west coast. Although the smaller population of New Zealand meant there were fewer obstacles to intermarriage and social mobility, Irish Catholics still faced many of the same disadvantages as they did in Australia and, to some extent, America: anti-Catholic prejudice, resentment against rural immigrants living in urban conditions, discrimination in housing and employment. As in America, these were ultimately overcome in Australia and New Zealand through growing power in the labour associations, the political parties, and the Church itself. Even at its height, however, it must be said that emigrants to Australia and New Zealand remained only a small fraction of the total numbers leaving the country in the nineteenth century.

Pre-Famine Emigration

The great flood of emigration which was permanently to alter the character of Ireland began in the early decades of the nineteenth century. Although many other factors contributed to it, the most fundamental underlying cause was population growth. At the start of the eighteenth century, the most reliable estimates put the total population of the country at around two million. By 1754 this had risen to only 2.3 million, a tiny rate of growth by contemporary standards, due to poverty, disease and Ulster emigration. By 1800, the number was between 4,500,000 and 5,000,000, in the 1821 census it was recorded as 6,800,000, and by 1841 it was 8,200,000. This increase was largely concentrated in the period from about 1780 to 1830, and overwhelmingly affected the poorest, labouring classes. What caused such rapid growth is still a matter of controversy, but some of the possible reasons are clear: traditionally, marriage ages in Ireland were relatively young, leading to very large families, and the subdivision of holdings enforced by the Penal Laws permitted increasing numbers to marry and stay on the land, albeit at the cost of a continually poorer standard of living. It seems clear as well that the relative prosperity brought about by rising prices during the period of the Napoleonic wars, from 1790 to 1814, encouraged early marriage, lowered infant mortality and made it possible for more people to exist off smaller holdings. At any rate, the stark fact is that over seventy or so years the population of the country almost quadrupled; since the vast majority were already living in the most abject poverty even before this increase, a disaster was clearly in the making.

In the aftermath of the Napoleonic wars, from 1814, came an immediate and dramatic economic slump: prices fell catastrophically, major industries collapsed, investment and growth stagnated, and unemployment and destitution became widespread. The depression lasted for almost two decades, and was accompanied by a series of natural catastrophes. In 1816-18, bad weather destroyed grain and potato crops, and smallpox and typhus killed over 50,000 people. The potato crop failed again in Munster in 1821, and people starved to death in Cork and Clare. After further crop failures in 1825-30, famine was only averted by the import of large amounts of Indian meal from America, and in 1832 'stark famine' struck Munster and south Leinster. Throughout the early 1830s cholera repeatedly ravaged the poorest classes and, in the decade as a whole, the potato crop failed on a local level in eight out of the ten years. There was a savage winter in 1838, and 'the night

of the big wind', in which snow buried the cottages and cattle froze to death in the fields. Finally, in 1840-44, the potato crops partly failed three more times. Small wonder that the Irish should feel God had abandoned them. 'There is a Distruction Approaching to Ireland', wrote one emigrant, 'their time is nerely at an end'.

From 1814, the shipping lanes to North America, which had been closed by the war, were reopened, and mass emigration restarted. In 1815-16 alone, over 20,000 crossed from Ireland to North America. At first, the pattern was very similar to the earlier migrations; about two-thirds of those leaving in the years 1815-19 were from Ulster, and many were people in the class above the very poorest – artisans, shopkeepers, 'strong' farmers and professionals – more often than not travelling in family groups. This was largely because British legislation discriminated against United States shipping, and thus kept the cost of passage prohibitively high. For the same reason, most of these emigrants went to British North America, rather than to the U.S.A., travelling in returning Canadian timber ships. The vast majority pushed on from Canada to the United States, where there were family or community links, although increasing numbers now began to stay in the rapidly expanding colony, often encouraged by government grants of land.

Over the course of the next two decades, as economic depression and natural disasters took their toll, the character of the emigration began to change. Despite the continuing high fares, more and more of those leaving were from the labouring classes, the poorest, who somehow managed prices for the passage ranging from £4 to £10 per person. Similarly, the religious make-up of those leaving was altering. More and more Catholics were now leaving, some assisted by such schemes as that briefly implemented by the British government in 1823-25, which provided free passage and land grants to over 2,500 Catholic smallholders, primarily from the Mallow and Fermoy districts of north Cork. The biggest single spur to such emigration, however, came in 1827, when the government repealed all restrictions on emigration; between 1828 and 1837 almost 400,000 Irish people left for North America. Up to 1832, about half of the emigrants still came from Ulster, but after that date the three southern provinces contributed the majority, and from now on, although a steady stream of Northern Protestants continued to emigrate, encouraged by the established Scots-Irish community, their proportion of total emigration was in continuous decline.

Up to the 1830s, the favoured route for the emigrants was still to Canada, and from there to the United States. The majority of departures were from Irish ports, with Belfast, Londonderry and Dublin now the most important. However, over the 1830s, as trade increased between Liverpool and the U.S., the cost of the the direct journey dropped, and increasing numbers crossed to Liverpool and from there made their way to New York, Boston and Philadelphia. For the very poorest Britain became the final destination; those who could not afford even the lower fares across the Atlantic paid the few pence for deck passage across the Irish sea. Conditions on such crossings were appalling. Deck passengers had a lower priority than baggage or livestock, and up to 2,000 people could be crowded onto an open deck in all weathers, clinging to each other to avoid being washed overboard. In 1830-35 200,000 Irish people made such crossings, and by 1841 over 400,000 lived permanently in Britain, mostly in the largest cities: Glasgow, London, Manchester, and Liverpool itself.

Between 1838 and 1844, the patterns were set which would make possible the massive Famine and post-Famine departures; large numbers of southern Catholic Irish left from all areas of the country, establishing both an example for the future and a community of sorts which could absorb new arrivals, and the Liverpool-New York route had become routine and relatively cheap. Although Ulster emigration continued, more emigrants now took ship at Cork than at Belfast, and large numbers also left from such ports as Limerick and Sligo. Many of those disembarking at Canadian and American ports are described as desperately poor, but in fact, even at this stage, the majority of those leaving did not come from the very poorest classes. Even in the 1840s officials and landlords continued to complain that those who were going were the 'better sort'. As one Protestant clergyman put it, 'the young, the enterprising and the industrious leave us, while the old, the idle and indolent portions, the dregs, stay with us.'

The old attitudes to emigration changed slowly in the years leading up to the Famine. At first, the old, negative view persisted. In the years after the end of the

and moving became less unknown and threatening. Even for those who thought of emigration as escape from economic and social oppression, however, there were severe cultural, social and even psychological problems; the rupture with the still powerfully influential traditions of extended community and family remained extremely painful for all who left.

The Famine

For the great mass of the people of Ireland, subsistence was made possible by one thing alone, the potato. Described by modern nutritionists as the one staple food capable of sustaining life as a sole diet, it had been common in Ireland since the seventeenth century, and was already at that point identified with Ireland in the eyes of some foreigners: anti-Irish mobs in seventeenth-century England are described as having used a potato impaled on a stick to represent the Irish. At that time, however, and during the early part of the eighteenth century, it formed only the basic part of a diet which also included milk, buttermilk, eggs, fish, and meat for the better-off. As the pressures of population grew through the last part of the eighteenth century and into the nineteenth century, for large numbers of people it went from being an important food to being the only food. Since a single acre of potatoes could feed a family of six, it was the basis of survival of the very poorest. Contemporary accounts describe the Irish eating huge quantities, an average, according to contemporary statistics, of ten pounds a day per person.

Partial failures of the potato crop, and resulting local famines, were relatively common up to the 1840s. In 1845, however, a previously unknown blight appeared without warning and destroyed the potatoes so rapidly that terror was spread throughout the countryside. 'The air was laden with a sickly odour of decay, as if the hand of death had stricken the potato field, and everything growing in it was rotten.' That year, only 30 to 40 per cent of the crop was actually destroyed, and though there was great suffering, few starved; people ate food normally sold to pay rent, pawned clothes, depended on public relief. All of these could only be temporary measures, and everything depended on the following year's crop. In late July and early August 1846 the blight returned, and this time, with astonishing rapidity, destroyed almost the entire potato crop. Less than one fifth of the harvest survived. In 1847, although

The pressure of world opinion did more to prompt British action than the needs of those who were starving. Help from the United States was practical as well as political; huge amounts of money were sent by earlier emigrants to help the departure of those still remaining.

Napoleonic wars, according to a Dublin newspaper, 'the native Irish' still held 'a vehement and, in many instances, an absurd attachment to the soil on which they were born.' This traditional hostility to emigration was strongest in those areas of the country where the old Gaelic traditions survived, on the western coasts and in other remote, mountainous regions, densely populated and suffering the greatest poverty. For these people, emigration was still banishment, still the greatest evil next to death. Even here, however, as the deprivations of the 1820s and 1830s deepened, some emigration occurred, although the great exodus from these areas did not come until the 1880s. In other, more anglicized districts of the country, emigrants' letters often painted an unrealistically bright picture of the life which awaited their friends and relatives across the Atlantic and, as more and more people left, the prospect of uprooting

the blight eased because so few potatoes were sown, the harvest was only ten per cent of the 1844 level. Encouraged by the relative healthiness of the 1847 crop, mass planting took place once more, but the blight returned in full force in 1848, with the countryside 'from sea to sea one mass of unvaried rottenness and decay'. Blight continued to ravage the crop for the following six years, and it was not until 1855 that the total harvest reached more than half of what it had been in 1844.

From the summer of 1846 on, the blight brought immediate and horrible distress. One historian estimates that between 1.1 and 1.5 million people died of starvation and famine-related diseases, and scenes of unimaginable mass suffering were witnessed: 'cowering wretches almost naked in the savage weather, prowling in turnip fields and endeavouring to grub up roots', 'famished and ghastly skeletons, such as no words can describe', 'little children, their limbs fleshless, their faces bloated, yet wrinkled and of a pale greenish hue'. Deaths were highest in south Ulster, west Munster and Connacht, those parts of the country where the population of poorest subsistence farmers and labourers was most dense, but very few areas escaped entirely; all over the country landless labourers died in their tens of thousands, and even shopkeepers, townspeople, and relatively comfortable farmers perished from the effects of the diseases spread by the starving and destitute.

Although the blight itself was unavoidable, its impact on Ireland was magnified by the response of the British government. Blinkered by free-market dogma, and by a profound, almost malevolent indifference to Irish ills, the government refused to recognize the scale of the disaster or to provide public assistance above the level existing before 1844. Only after the horrors of the winter of 1847, when world opinion made it impossible to ignore the magnitude of the cataclysm occurring in Ireland, were efforts finally made to organize public relief. Even then, these efforts were hampered by slavish adherence to the ideals of the free-marketeers: the poor could not be allowed to become dependent on the state and, above all, the market itself should not be interfered with. As a result, thousands of starving people were put to work, for barely enough to keep them alive from day to day, on projects with no practical value, such as unnecessary bridges, and roads that led from nowhere to nowhere.

Famine Emigration

The effect of the Great Famine on emigration was immediate and dramatic. Between 1845 and 1855, almost 1.5 million people embarked for the United States; 340,000 sailed for British North America; around 300,000 settled in the cities of Great Britain, and about 70,000 went to Australia. In all, more than 2.1 million people left Ireland in these eleven years, over a quarter of the pre-Famine population, and greater than the combined total of all those who had left in the previous two-and-a-half centuries. Together with the huge Famine death-rate among children, the result was the disappearance of almost an entire generation: less than one in three of those born in the early 1830s died in Ireland of old age.

To some extent the enormous wave of Famine emigration followed earlier patterns. Those districts which were poor but not utterly destitute – east Connacht, south Ulster and the Leinster midlands – contributed the greatest numbers. Areas like west Cork and south Londonderry, densely populated by the poorest subsistence farmers, suffered appalling death rates, while east Cork and north Londonderry, relatively more prosperous, lost huge numbers through emigration. Only north Connacht experienced simultaneously high rates of death and emigration. Nevertheless, there were significant differences from earlier migrations. Whereas only 60 per cent of those arriving at New York were classed as 'labourers' in 1836, by 1851-55 the proportion had risen to between 79 and 90 per cent. More than ever before, these people needed financial assistance to pay for the crossing, and this generally came from relatives. A family would combine their money, or borrow, to send one son or cousin to the U.S., he would then send back money to bring out another member of the family, and in this way, little by little, entire families, or even communities, would manage to get away. A huge amount of money poured into Ireland from America, particularly in the early 1850s, to be used to finance the departure of further emigrants.

A change also came about in the prevailing attitudes to emigration. Where previously there had been at least some measure of choice in the decision to leave, and pain at the breaking of communal ties, the dominant note now was desperation, panic even. Most earlier emigrants had been sensitive to reports of hard times in

Emigrants leaving Queenstown (now Cobh) for New York in 1874. The introduction of steamships on the Atlantic route dramatically reduced the length, and the horrors, of the journey.

the U.S. and difficulties in the journey; now the exodus continued to grow even in the face of the most discouraging reports from abroad and the savage hardships of a mid-winter Atlantic crossing. As one group pleaded, 'all we want is to get out of Ireland, we must be better anywhere than here'. Despair was the driving force in a panic-stricken scramble for survival.

Desperation was also reflected in the changing routes for emigration. Previously, passengers had embarked at the major ports in Ireland, or from Liverpool. Now emigrant ships left from small, little-used ports such as Westport, Kinsale and Killala. Some idea of the conditions endured by the people on board such ships can be gleaned from the story of one, the *Elizabeth and Sarah*, which left Killala in May 1847. The vessel, built in

1763, was 83 years old, and carried 276 passengers, 121 more than the legal limit. For all these people there were only 36 berths. During the voyage, no food was given to the passengers, who had to rely on whatever they had managed to bring on board, and a maximum of only two pints of water per person per day was allocated. When she arrived off Quebec, after a journey of 41 days, all the water on board was unfit to drink, 18 people, including the master of the ship, had died of fever and the remainder were starving. In some respects, considering the condition of the ship, those who survived were lucky: on some of the 'coffin ships' the death rates were 30 per cent and more. For those attempting to use the Liverpool route, as well as overcrowding, starvation and disease, the dangers included unscrupulous middlemen and landlords, thieves, conmen, and the extortionate tactics of ships' agents and owners. Still, with the only alternative a slow death at home, hundreds of thousands faced and overcame these horrifying obstacles.

Young Irish-Americans watching the St Patrick's Day parade,
still a display of pride in both homelands, old and new.

Clans and Families of Ireland

Irish America and the Effects of Emigration

The experience of the Famine emigrants in America was also different from that of their predecessors. The sheer scale of the influx flooded the labour market, leaving the vast majority of the newcomers clustered together in poverty in ghettoes in the cities of the east coast: New York, Philadelphia and Boston. In New York City in 1850, 30,000 people, most of them Irish, were living below ground level in cellars often flooded by rainwater or sewage. Such work as there was, for example on the construction of the Erie canal and the railroads, tended to be harsh and poorly paid, and traditional animosity towards Irish Catholics resulted in institutional

A pipe band plays before a hurling match. The late nineteenth-century revival of sport and culture was only possible with Irish-American support.

discrimination and injustice: mob violence, underpaid (or unpaid) wages, 'No Irish Need Apply' notices, these were the common experience for the decades up to the 1870s. Significant numbers of those who emigrated simply failed to survive; one Irish-American wrote that 'the average life of an emigrant after landing here is six years, and many insist it is much less'. Certainly, it was only after 1870 that Irish-American society began to

coalesce and stabilize, finding protection and strength through the institutions of the Catholic Church and the Democratic Party, and even then a large minority of Irish-Americans remained amongst the poorest and most deprived.

From the 1870s on, Irish-America had a voice, not only in the United States itself, but also in the politics of Ireland. Large numbers of Irish-Americans simply blamed Britain for having forced them to emigrate, seeing their departure as a direct result of political oppression, rather than economic necessity, and the very real British mismanagement and indifference during the Famine left a legacy of intense bitterness which found expression in fervent support for the successive nationalist movements of the late nineteenth and early twentieth centuries. Such Irish-American societies as Clan na Gael in the 1870s, the National League of

America in the 1880s, and de Valera's American Association for the Recognition of the Irish Republic in 1919-21 played a vital role in providing support for the Land League, the Fenians, the Home Rule movement and Sinn Féin in Ireland itself. It is doubtful if any of the changes brought about by these movements, including the ultimate independence of the 26 southern counties in 1921, could have been achieved without the moral and financial backing of Irish-America. Such backing continues right up to the present.

In America itself, the Irish played a part that was almost equally important. The close community ties which the emigrants brought with them provided the basis for a tightly organized political machine which, through the Democratic Party, achieved local power and then increasing national influence until, by 1963, the President, the Speaker of the House of

Representatives, the Majority Leader of the Senate, and the Chairman of the National Committee were all Irish-American Catholic Democrats. With political power came relative wealth and increasing assimilation. As growing prosperity allowed the Irish to move out of ghetto areas the old ties weakened, but the general characteristics of their culture remained: hardworking and materialist, socially conservative, family-centred, and with a great residue of nostalgia for Ireland itself.

Post-Famine Emigration

In the history of other nations, such catastrophes as the Famine have slowed the growth of the population only temporarily. In Ireland's case, however, the great explosion of emigration during the Famine years simply accelerated a trend already present; the total population declined from around 8.5 million in 1845 to 5.8 million in 1861, and continued to shrink, to less than 4.3 million in 1926. In the 80 years before 1926, the country lost an estimated 4.1 million inhabitants to emigration. Somewhere between half a million and a million went to Great Britain, to the South Wales coalfields and the great industrial metropolises of Scotland and England. Many of these eventually joined the vast majority, over three million, who went directly to the United States, so that the total for American emigration probably reaches more than three-and-a-half million for these years. Of the rest, around 200,000 went to Canada, almost 300,000 to Australia and New Zealand, and another 60,000 or so to Argentina, South Africa and other destinations. The U.S., though, was the overwhelming choice of the emigrants; by 1900 it contained more Irish than Ireland itself.

The reasons for the continued vast migration are, on the face of it, varied. The American Civil War produced a large demand for manpower in the early 1860s, particularly in the industries and army of the North; over 200,000 Irishmen fought in the war, the overwhelming majority for the North, and many of these were recruited in Ireland by agents who offered free passage and substantial bounties (by Irish standards). The journey itself began to hold fewer terrors, as steamships cut the travelling time, competition reduced fares and government regulation improved conditions on board. In America, the growing power of the Irish-American community afforded some welcome protection from the uncertainties of starting a

new life. In Ireland there was an increasing determination not to subdivide further small family farms, which meant that only one son could expect to stay. But the single most important factor in sustaining the flood of emigration was economic deprivation. Mass evictions, the near-famines of 1861-64 and 1879-82, the continual

Facing page: the Gaelic Society's hurling and football team, which played throughout the northeastern U.S. in 1890-2. Above: Sunday morning Mass for Irish-American soldiers of the Union in Arlington, Virginia, in 1861.

grinding poverty of subsistence farming; these ensured that for the vast majority any opportunity to improve their lives would be gladly welcomed, and the improved ease of emigration simply made it possible for many to take that opportunity.

Emigration in these years also affected areas which had previously remained relatively immune. The most traditional areas of the country, still Irish-speaking, had suffered terrible death-rates in the Famine and its aftermath, but maintained the old resistance to the idea of emigration. The crisis of 1879-82 had a decisive impact on these areas, and that resistance collapsed: a flood of departures began from Kerry, west Cork, west Galway, Mayo and Donegal. 'The full conviction had come upon them,' wrote one observer 'that it was impossible to struggle longer with the depth of poverty by which they had been surrounded.' Between 1881 and

1901 the number of Irish-speakers in Munster and Connacht fell by a third.

The flood to the U.S. continued until the First World War, when shipping was severely disrupted, then resumed, reaching a peak in the years from 1921 to 1923, and finally began to decline. After this, North America ceased to be the most important destination; international depression, American restrictions on immigrants, and the simple fact of population depletion limited the numbers of those departing, and a growing British demand for labour up to the 1960s, together with

As their prosperity and influence grew, the Irish in America retained a strong sense of community, as shown in these pictures taken at the turn of the century in Refugio Co., Texas. Right: Oscar Fagan outside his farmhouse. Below: the Irish gather after Mass.

Throughout the late nineteenth and early twentieth centuries emigration continued to weaken rural communities, and in some cases ultimately destroyed them. The Blasket Islands, Co. Kerry (above) were abandoned by their last inhabitants only in 1953.

the relative ease of transport back and forth between the two islands, meant that Britain now received by far the greatest number of emigrants. The population of the 26 counties of the Republic, around three million in 1921, continued to shrink, to 2.8 million in 1961. It is only in the last two decades that this trend has been reversed, with the current population around 3.5 million. Although it had been hoped that the necessity for emigration had been banished, the last years of the 1980s saw a growth again in the departures of the young to the U.S. and Britain. It seems likely, however, that this is only a temporary phenomenon.

For Northern Ireland the picture is slightly different. Since the creation of the state in 1921, the population has grown from around 1.3 to 1.5 million. This increase reflects the relatively greater prosperity of the area, due to earlier industrialization and better integration into the economy of Great Britain. The increase would be larger were it not for continuing emigration. In the early years of the state, this consisted mostly of Catholics leaving for the U.S., many of them embittered by the outcome of the struggle with the British, the creation of Northern Ireland itself. On the Protestant side, emigration was, and continues to be, almost exclusively to the former British dominions of Canada and Australia; from the end of the nineteenth century these have been favoured over the U.S., principally because of the existence in these places of the strong family and community links provided by such institutions as the Orange Order, but also because the size and power of

the Catholic Irish-American influence in the U.S. made it less attractive. With the restrictions placed on immigration by Australia, New Zealand and Canada from the 1960s, this emigration too has now slowed to a trickle.

The Effects of Emigration

The vast exodus of people from Ireland through the nineteenth and into the twentieth century changed the character of the country permanently. This is apparent even on a purely physical level in the appearance of much of Ireland today: the magnificent emptiness of the bogs and mountains of the west, the crumbling, deserted villages, the unspoilt countryside – these are all a direct result of the enforced departure of so many. From being one of the European countries with the highest density of population in the early nineteenth century, Ireland has now become the most thinly populated, with an average number of people per square mile only one tenth that of England. And, since most of the population is now concentrated in the cities of the east coast, this average actually underestimates the emptiness of the rest of the country.

The profound demoralization caused by the Famine and its aftermath produced a widespread feeling that the country was finished, that it could not survive, and this in turn had a dramatic effect on the old, Gaelic culture. To take one aspect only, the Irish language was spoken by around two million people in 1851; by 1971, the official figure was 70,000. The old language was associated with poverty, deprivation and despair; it became identified with failure, of which emigration was overwhelmingly visible proof. Despite heroic efforts to save and revive the language it has now almost disappeared as a living tongue, and at a rate unparalleled in recent European history.

Perhaps the clearest positive effect of emigration, and the resulting creation of large Irish communities overseas, has been an early and sophisticated awareness in Ireland of the country's position in the world. The unique situation of being the first part of the British Empire to become independent, as well as being the only western European country to have been a victim, rather than a practitioner, of imperialism, has given Ireland a role in world affairs out of all proportion to her size, a role supported and made possible by the continuing connections with the overseas Irish.

These pages: the effects of emigration are evident in the Irish countryside even today, in the poignantly unspoilt beauty and the abandoned, decaying cottages.

Above and facing page: the hand-made Book of the
Boyles, showing the descent of the Anglo-Irish Earls of
Cork and Orrery, is a masterpiece of heraldic art.

Clans and Families of Ireland

Heraldry and Ireland

Heraldry is the study and description ('blazoning') of coats of arms, and of the rights of individuals and families to bear arms. It has its origins in the first half of the twelfth century, when knights in continental Europe first began to use markings on their shields to identify themselves in battles and in tournaments. This became necessary because of developments in medieval weaponry and armour. Coats of chain-and-link mail, with long shields, gave way to full-body plate armour and helmets encasing the entire head, with smaller triangular shields. As a result, the individual was completely anonymous; the urgency of knowing whether the large, armour-clad individual galloping at you was a friend or an enemy is self-evident.

At first, military necessity was paramount. Large, clearly identifiable patterns, involving two or three colours divided into a number of compartments related to the physical construction of the shield make up the earliest arms. Later, when animals and other symbols were added, the necessity for easy, quick recognition again meant that a large degree of stylised convention was used, so that the heraldic lion, for instance, bears only a slight resemblance to the real thing.

The military origin of arms is also the most likely

explanation for their emergence at almost exactly the same time in England, France, Germany and Italy. The eight Christian crusades against Islam between 1096 and 1271 involved knights from all of these countries, and, combined with the changes in armour, provided a context in which a system of military recognition was essential. The endurance of heraldry is no doubt partly due to the fact that it spread over the whole of Europe virtually simultaneously. Crosses and fleurs-de-lys, Christian symbols *par excellence*, also take their origins in heraldry from the Crusades.

But heraldry would long ago have died out completely if the only need it met was military. Individual recognition and family identity are both powerful and universal human needs and, towards the end of the thirteenth century, a further change came about as the social and non-military aspects of heraldry evolved and it became established that coats of arms were personal and hereditary. The symbols used could now relate to the name, the office or the territory of the bearer, and were dictated less by the imperative of immediate recognition. One of the results from this period on was the creation of so-called 'canting' arms, based on a pun on the name – in Ireland, the arms of the Aherne family, displaying three herons, are an example. The main non-military use of arms was on seals, as a means of proving the authenticity of documents, and the practice of using birds or animals to fill empty space around the arms on these seals gave rise to 'supporters', now regarded as part of the arms of peers. Eventually, arms were also used on tombs, and then on works of art and possessions.

The symbols used in heraldry have a variety of origins: in the Christian nature of the crusades, in the (supposed) character of the individual or family itself, in some event which is identified with the family. There is no strict attachment of significance to particular symbols, although the reasons for some symbols are self-evident; the lion is conventionally regal, the unicorn is a symbol of purity, the boar is a Celtic symbol of endurance and courage, and so on.

As arms proliferated, a natural need arose for rules to prevent different individuals and families using the same or similar symbols and arrangements of symbols. The first result was the evolution of the peculiar technical vocabulary used in describing arms, a highly stylised and extremely precise mixture of early French, Latin and English, still used in heraldry today. Then came the creation of the offices of King of Arms or King of Heralds throughout most of Europe in the fourteenth century. The principal functions of these were the recognition of arms, the recording of the possession of arms, the granting of arms and adjudication in disputes between bearers of arms. By the end of the fifteenth century, since the right to bear arms depended on family and ancestry, they had also become genealogists.

Irish Heraldic Traditions

Arms first arrived in Ireland with the Normans, who brought with them all the social structures on which European heraldry depended; up to then, although some evidence of the use of military symbolism among the Gaels survives, heraldry in the true sense did not exist. Norman heraldry shows clearly its military origins, with a preponderance of clear, simple devices, (known as 'ordinaries') designed for easy recognition. Examples of these are found in the arms of the de Burgos, de Clares, Fitzgeralds and other families of Norman extraction.

A separate heraldic tradition is found in the arms of the Anglo-Irish. This can be dated to the mid-sixteenth century, when the Tudor monarchs of England began to address themselves seriously to taking possession of Ireland, and establishing the full panoply of English law. Accordingly, the Office of Ulster King of Arms, with authority over all arms in Ireland, was set up in 1552 as part of the household of the Vice-Regal Court, the administration of the English King's deputy in Ireland. Inevitably, the early records of the Office contain many examples of Anglo-Irish heraldic practice, characterised by great elaboration, with individual shields often containing as many as a dozen charges, reflecting the preoccupations of the Anglo-Irish with family relationships. Whereas Norman arms are clearly military, the arms of the Anglo-Irish are part of a much more settled society, concerned above all about status.

The third tradition of heraldry in Ireland relates to the original inhabitants, the Gaelic Irish, and is more problematic, since heraldry was a natural aspect of the social life of both Normans and Anglo-Irish, but originally had no part in Gaelic society. The characteristics of the arms in use among the important Gaelic families do have a number of common features, however. In part this is due to the role of genealogy in early Irish society;

Heraldic banners showing the arms of the O'Neills (above) and the MacCarthys (above right). The red hand, now used as the symbol of Ulster, and the stag, common in the arms of many Munster families, have their origins in pre-Christian Ireland.

the myth of a common origin was a potent means of unifying the different Celtic and pre-Celtic peoples of Ireland, and the enormously elaborate Gaelic pseudo-genealogies, tracing every family in the country back to the same individual, were designed to reinforce that myth. In addition, on a more mundane level the nature of Gaelic law meant that, in effect, what you could own depended on who you were related to. These two factors, the importance of the origin myth and the property rights of the extended family, are reflected in the heraldic tradition which grew up in Ireland from about the fifteenth century.

Unlike the military simplicity of the Normans or the conventional elaborations of the Anglo-Irish, the symbols used in the arms of Gaelic Irish families tend to relate to pre-Christian myths, often in quite obscure ways. Thus, for example, the Red Hand of the O'Neills,

now also associated with the province of Ulster, in heraldic terms *a dexter hand appaumé gules*, also occurs in various forms in the arms of other Gaelic families. The reason would appear to lie in the name of the son of Bolg or Nuadu, the Celtic sun-god, in some accounts the divine ancestor of all the Celts. This son was known as Labraid Lámhdhearg, or 'Labraid of the Red Hand'. The association with the ancestral power of the sun-god is clearly a very good reason for the choice of symbol.

In a similar way, the stag which appears in the arms of many Munster families – MacCarthy, O'Sullivan, Healy and many others – relates very clearly to the kingship myth of the Érainn peoples. In this myth, the legitimacy of the ruling house is confirmed when a stag enters; the animal is hunted, and the border of the territory is defined by the chase; the future ruler is the individual who eventually slays the stag. What the many families displaying the stag in their arms have in common is that they were originally part of the great Eoghanacht tribal grouping which dominated Munster until the time of Brian Boru. The stag was self-evidently an appropriate choice of symbol.

Above: the oak in the arms of the O'Conors is an old symbol of kingship.

As in Ulster and Munster, so in Connacht the arms of the ruling family, the O'Conors, and of a whole host of others connected with them – Flanagan, O'Beirne and many more – all display a common symbol, in this case the oak tree. Again, the reason lies in pre-Christian belief, in the old Celtic reverence for the oak, and its resulting association with kingship; the medieval sources record ruling families having at least one sacred tree outside the family's ring-fort.

As well as the association of heraldic symbolism with pre-Christian myth, the nature of the property relations within the extended family meant that arms were used in ways quite different from those practised among the Normans and Anglo-Irish. In particular, most of the arms were regarded as the property of the sept (defined by Dr Edward MacLysaght as 'a group of persons inhabiting the same locality and bearing the same surname'), rather than being strictly hereditary within a single family, as was and is the case under English and Scottish heraldic law.

In summary, two of the three heraldic traditions in Ireland, the Norman and the Anglo-Irish, form part of the mainstream of European heraldry, while the arms found among the Gaelic Irish have particular characteristics which set them apart.

The Genealogical Office

The Genealogical Office is the successor to the Office of Ulster King of Arms which, as noted above, was created in 1552 with full jurisdiction over arms in Ireland. Ulster retained this power for almost four centuries, until 1943, when the title was transferred to the College of Arms in London and the office of Chief Herald of Ireland

Above: Herald's tabard, part of the uniform of the Office of Ulster King of Arms on ceremonial occasions. Embroidered on it are the British Royal Arms.

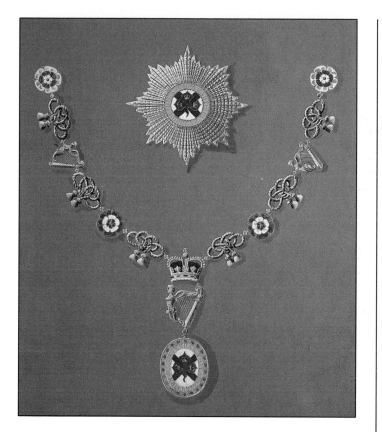

Above: the insignia of the chivalric Order of St Patrick. Founded in the eighteenth century to be an Irish equivalent of such English institutions as the Orders of the Bath and the Garter, it is now defunct.

was created to continue to fulfil the functions of Ulster in independent Ireland. The new name given to the Office of the Chief Herald, 'The Genealogical Office', was somewhat inaccurate, since its primary concern continues to be heraldic rather than genealogical.

Over the first 150 years of its existence, the Office was almost exclusively concerned with Anglo-Irish heraldry, recording, registering and legitimising the practice of arms that had grown up. From the start of the eighteenth century Ulster began to acquire other duties, as an officer of the crown intimately linked to the government. These duties were largely ceremonial, deciding and arranging precedence on state occasions, as well as introducing new peers to the Irish House of Lords and recording peerage successions. When the chivalric Order of St Patrick was introduced in 1783 as an Irish equivalent of such long-established English institutions as the Order of the Garter, Ulster became its

registrar, responsible for administering its affairs. He also continued to have responsibility for the ceremonial aspects of state occasions at the court of the English Viceroy. The heraldic and ceremonial duties of Ulster continued down to the twentieth century.

Today the Office of the Chief Herald remains principally concerned with the granting of arms to individuals and corporate bodies, the ceremonial aspect having lapsed with the establishment of the Republic of Ireland. One aspect of the Office's work today is perhaps connected to this, however. This is the practice of recognising Chiefs of the Name, instituted in the 1940s by Dr Edward MacLysaght, the first Chief Herald. The aim was simply to acknowledge the descendants of the leading Gaelic Irish families, and this was done by uncovering the senior descendants in the male line of the last Chief of the Name duly inaugurated as such under the old Gaelic laws. The practice is a courtesy only; under Irish law no hereditary titles are recognised.

One final aspect of the contemporary Genealogical Office is worthy of mention. This is the State Heraldic Museum, established in 1909 by Sir Neville Wilkinson, then Ulster, and continued by his successors, including the present Chief Herald. Now housed in what was the old Kildare St Club, the Museum shows the diversity of arms in use in Ireland, as well as demonstrating the variety of uses to which heraldic designs have been put, including livery buttons, postage stamps, heraldic banners, signet rings, coins and notes, corporate and county arms, bookbinding, heraldic china and porcelain and much more. It is a permanent reminder that heraldry retains an important and familiar place even today.

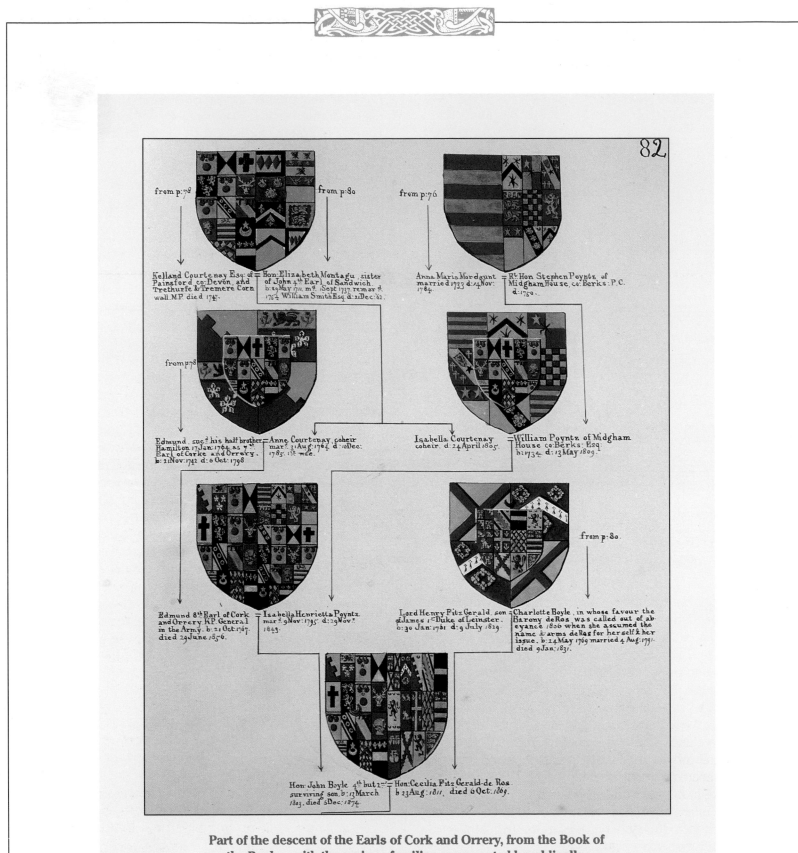

from p:78   from p:80   from p:76

Kelland Courtenay Esq: of = Hon: Elizabeth Montagu, sister   Anna Maria Mordaunt = Rt. Hon Stephen Poyntz, of
Painsford co: Devon, and   of John 4th Earl of Sandwich.   married 1733 d: 4 Nov: Midgham House, co: Berks: P.C.
Trethurfe & Tremere Corn   b: 29 May 1711 m.d 1 Sept 1737 remar d   1784.   d: 1750.
wall. M.P died 1747.   1754 William Smith Esq: d: 21 Dec: '62.

from p:78

Edmund, sucd his half brother = Anne Courtenay, coheir   Isabella Courtenay = William Poyntz, of Midgham
Hamilton 17 Jan: 1764. as 7th   mar.d 31 Aug: 1764 d: 10 Dec: coheir d: 24 April 1805.   House co: Berks: Esq:
Earl of Corke and Orrery.   1785. 1st wife.   b: 1734. d: 13 May 1809.
b: 21 Nov: 1742 d: 6 Oct: 1798

                                                                                          from p: 80.

Edmund 8th Earl of Cork = Isabella Henrietta Poyntz.   Lord Henry FitzGerald, son = Charlotte Boyle, in whose favour the
and Orrery. K.P. General mar.d 9 Nov: 1795. d: 29 Nov.d   of James 1st Duke of Leinster.   Barony de Ros was called out of ab-
in the Army. b: 21 Oct: 1767. 1843.   b: 30 Jan: 1761 d: 9 July 1829.   eyance 1806 when she assumed the
died 29 June 1856.   name & arms de Ros for herself & her
                                                                                           issue. b: 24 May 1769 married 4 Aug: 1791.
                                                                                           died 9 Jan: 1831.

Hon: John Boyle, 4th but 2d = Hon: Cecilia Fitz Gerald-de Ros.
surviving son. b: 13 March   b: 23 Aug: 1811, died 6 Oct: 1869.
1803, died 5 Dec: 1874.

**Part of the descent of the Earls of Cork and Orrery, from the Book of
the Boyles, with the various families represented heraldically.**

Clans and Families of Ireland

Clans and Families of Ireland

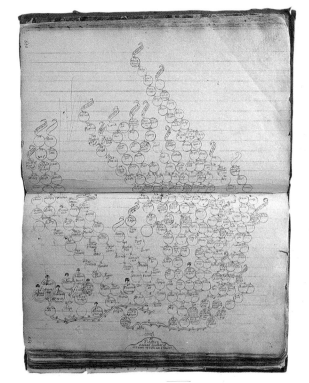

The history of Ireland is a great drama of war, invasion, plantation, immigration, emigration, conflict and solidarity. Like all history, however, it is composed of countless individual family histories, each unique. Surnames are the point where history and family history intersect, marking individuality and kinship.

The intermingling of cultures in Ireland – Gaelic, Viking, Norman, British – has created a huge number of surnames and left ambiguity surrounding the origins of many of them, an ambiguity that is itself an feature of Irishness. No description of Irish families and their surnames can afford to ignore this by selecting only those that

Above: the descent of the *Uí Fiachrach*, from Roger O'Ferrall's *Linea Antiqua*. The semi-historical Fiachra is at the bottom, and the various families and offshoots, including the Madigans, O'Hanlons and Moonys, grow upwards and outwards.

match the history of one part of the island or the population.

What follows is an account of the two hundred or so most common surnames in Ireland today, chosen purely because they are the most common, and therefore including many which are more usually seen as English or Scottish. Any surname borne by an Irish person, whatever its origin, is an Irish surname.

77

AHERNE

Aherne is an anglicisation of *Ó hEachthianna*, from *Eachthiarna,* meaning 'lord of horses', and is also found in the variants 'Hearn' and 'Hearne'. *Eachthiarna* was a relatively common personal name in Gaelic society, borne by, for instance a brother of Brian Boru. The surname originated, in fact, in the sept or tribe of Brian, the *Dál gCais*, and has always been strongly associated with their homeland in Co. Clare. The family territory

AHERNE

was in the southeast of the county, around Sixmilebridge, up to the end of the Middle Ages, when they migrated south and east, to counties Cork, Limerick and Waterford. To this day, Ahernes are most numerous in counties Cork and Waterford.

The arms of the family include three herons, in an obvious pun on the name.

ALLEN

The name has two quite distinct origins, one Scots Gaelic, the other French. *Ailín*, meaning 'little rock', is the root of the Scottish name, originally MacAllan. The first recorded arrivals bearing the Scottish name came in the fifteenth century, as hired soldiers ('gallowglasses') imported to Donegal by the O'Donnells, and the migrations of the following two centuries brought many more.

In other cases, the surname derives from the old Breton personal name *Alan*, which in turn came from the Germanic tribal name *Alemannus*, meaning 'all men'. The same root provided the modern French name for Germany, *Allemagne*. Followers of the invading Normans were the first to carry the Breton version of the name to Ireland.

Irish families bearing the name may be of either origin, though the fact that two-thirds of the Allens are to be found in Ulster – they are especially numerous in counties Antrim and Armagh – suggests that the majority are of Scottish extraction.

ARMSTRONG

This surname originates in the area along the western Scottish borders; the first recorded bearer was Adam Armstrong, pardoned in Carlisle in 1235 for causing another man's death. They were among the most notorious of the riding Border clans, who also included the Elliots, the Grahams and the Johnstons, famous for

The Armstrong tartan

BARRETT   BARRY

their lawlessness and plunder. When the power of these clans was savagely broken after 1603 by James I, the Armstrongs scattered, and many migrated to Ulster, where a large number settled in Co. Fermanagh. Even today, Fermanagh is home to the largest concentration of Armstrong families in Ireland, although the name is quite common throughout Ulster, particularly in counties Antrim and Tyrone.

As well as those of Scottish origin, however, a good number of Irish Armstrongs are of Gaelic Irish extraction. Many of the Trin-Laverys of Co. Antrim and the Trainors of counties Tyrone and Monaghan had their surnames mis-translated as Armstrong, from the presence of the Irish for 'strong', *tréan*, in their original names.

BARRETT

The name Barrett is now concentrated in two widely separated parts of Ireland, in Co. Cork and in the Mayo-Galway region. The Irish version of the name is *Baróid* in the south and *Bairéid* in the west, and this may reflect two separate origins. At any rate, families of the surname

first appeared in these areas in the thirteenth century, after the Anglo-Norman invasion. Its Norman origin derives it from the old Germanic personal name, Bernard or Beraud. A separate derivation gives its origin as the Middle English 'Barat', a nickname for a quarrelsome or deceitful person.

The western family, originally based around Killala in Mayo, were thoroughly absorbed into Gaelic society very quickly, and in the Middle Ages began to split into various sub-clans, among them McAndrew, Timmons, and Roberts. The Cork settlers were not so Gaelicised, giving their name to the large barony of Barretts in the middle of the county.

The arms of the family are based on word play, a pictorial version of *barrettes*, French for 'short bars'.

BARRY

The first bearer of the surname to arrive in Ireland was Robert de Barri, one of the original band of Norman knights who landed at Bannow in Co. Wexford in May 1169, and a brother of Giraldus Cambrensis, historian of

The American tartan of Clan Bell

the invasion. The name comes from the earlier association of the family with the island of Barry, seven miles southwest of Cardiff in Wales. From the start the family were prominent in the settlement of east Cork, and were soon absorbed into the native culture, forming subsepts on Gaelic lines, the most important being Barry Mór, Barry Óg and Barry Roe. The names of two of these are perpetuated in the names of the Cork baronies of Barrymore and Barryroe, and many other Cork placenames are linked to the family: Kilbarry, Rathbarry and Buttevant (from the family motto *Boutez en avant*), to mention only three. The surname is now very numerous in Ireland, but still inextricably associated with Co. Cork.

As well as the Norman origin, two relatively uncommon Gaelic surnames, *Ó Beargha* and *Ó Báire,* have also been anglicised as Barry.

BEATTY

In Ulster, where it is found most frequently by far, this surname is generally of Scottish origin. In Scotland it originated as 'Baty', a pet form of Bartholomew. The family were well known in Galloway and along the Borders, where they were one of the infamous 'riding clans'. After the destruction by James I of these clans, many Beatties migrated to Ulster during the Plantation. Their settlements were concentrated especially in Co. Fermanagh, where they remain numerous.

Some Beatties, outside Ulster, also have a separate Gaelic origin, from *Mac Biataigh*, meaning 'provider of food'. The same original was also sometimes transliterated as Betagh.

BELL

The surname is one of the 100 most common in Ireland, and is found most frequently by far in the northern part of the country, particularly in Ulster, where it is especially numerous in counties Antrim and Down.

In Ulster, Bell is almost always of Scottish origin, the family being one of the infamous 'riding clans' along the Borders, descended from Gilbert le fitz Bel, *bel* meaning 'beautiful' or 'handsome'. After the destruction of the

power of these clans in the early seventeenth century, many Bells migrated to Ulster during the Plantation.

The name may also, more rarely, be a phonetic anglicisation of the Scots Gaelic *Mac Gille Mhaoil*, which was also turned into MacIlveil and MacGilveil.

BOYD

This surname originated in Scotland, and is now most common in Ulster, particularly in counties Antrim and Down. Two separate derivations are claimed for the name. The most commonly accepted links it with the Scottish island of Bute in the Firth of Clyde, in Gaelic *Bód*; the Gaelic for 'of Bute' is *Bóid*. Another derivation connects the family with the Stewarts, claiming that the descent is from Robert, son of Simon, one of the Norman founders of the Scottish Stewarts. Robert was known as *Buidhe*, meaning 'yellow', from the colour of his hair, and this is taken as the origin of the surname. Whatever the truth, the earliest recorded bearers of the name certainly used the Norman prefix *de*. These were Robertus de Boyde of Irvine and Alan de Bodha of Dumfries, both living in the early thirteenth century.

BOYLE

The Boyd tartan

BOYLE

Boyle, or O'Boyle, is now one of the fifty most common surnames in Ireland. In Irish the name is *Ó Baoghill*, the derivation of which is uncertain, but thought to be connected to the Irish *geall*, meaning 'pledge'. In the Middle Ages the family were powerful and respected, sharing control of the entire northwest of the island with the O'Donnells and the O'Dohertys, and the strongest association of the family is still with Co. Donegal, where (O)Boyle is the third most numerous name in the county.

The majority of those bearing the name are of Gaelic origin, but many Irish Boyles have separate, Norman origins. In Ulster, a significant number are descended from the Scottish Norman family of de Boyville, whose name comes from the town now known as Beauville in

Normandy. The most famous Irish family of the surname were the Boyles, Earls of Cork and Shannon, descended from Richard Boyle, who arrived in Ireland from Kent in 1588 and quickly amassed enormous wealth. His earliest known ancestor was Humphrey de Binville, a Norman lord in Herefordshire in the eleventh century.

BRADLEY

Although Bradley is a common English surname, derived from the many places in England so called, in Ireland the vast majority of Bradleys are in fact descended from the *Ó Brolcháin* sept. How English ears could have heard this as the equivalent of 'Bradley' remains one of the many little mysteries of Anglo-Irish relations. *Brollach*, the root of the name, means 'breast'.

The name originated in Co. Tyrone, and the territory inhabited by *Ó Brolcháin* families covered the area where the present-day counties of Tyrone, Derry and Donegal meet. From early times they appear to have migrated widely; one branch established itself in the Western Highlands of Scotland, while another settled in Co. Cork. The many Bradleys in that county to this day descend from this branch. Despite their travels, however, most Bradley families in Ireland today still live in their northern ancestral homeland.

BRADY

The surname derives from the Irish *Mac Brádaigh*, coming, possibly, from *brádach*, meaning 'thieving' or 'dishonest'. The name is among the sixty most frequently found in Ireland, and remains very numerous in Co. Cavan, their original homeland, with large numbers also to be found in the adjoining county of Monaghan. Their power was centred on an area a few miles east of Cavan town, from where they held jurisdiction over a large territory within the old Gaelic kingdom of Breifne. There have been many notable poets, clergymen and soldiers of the name, including Thomas Brady (1752-1827), a field marshal in the Austrian army, the satirical Gaelic poet Rev. Philip MacBrady, as well as three MacBrady Bishops of Kilmore, and one MacBrady Bishop of Ardagh. The pre-Reformation Cavan Crozier, originally belonging to one of these MacBradys, is now to be found in the National Museum in Dublin.

BRADY

BREEN

There are several distinct Gaelic origins of the surname, both *Mac Braoin* and *Ó Braoin*, from *braon*, meaning 'moisture', or 'drop'. The *Mac Braoin* were originally located near the town of Knocktopher in Co. Kilkenny, but migrated to Wexford after the Anglo-Norman invasions in the twelfth and thirteenth centuries. Co. Wexford is still the area of the country in which the

The arms of Athlone town, situated in the heart of the ancient homeland of the Breens.

BRENNAN

surname is most common, though a separate Wexford sept, the *Ó Briain*, also had their surname anglicised as Breen. These were descended from Bran Finn, son of Lachta, King of Munster, and uncle of Brian Boru. However, the O'Breens, rulers of Brawney, a territory near Athlone in counties Offaly and Westmeath, were the most powerful of the name in the Middle Ages; as they lost power the name mutated, and many in the area are now to be found as O'Briens. The surname is now also quite common in north Connacht, Co. Fermanagh, and in Co. Kerry.

BRENNAN

This is one of the most frequent surnames in Ireland and is to be found throughout the country, though noticeably less common in Ulster. It derives from the two Irish originals *Ó Braonáin* and *Mac Branáin* . The *Mac Branáin* were chiefs of a large territory in the east of the present Co. Roscommon, and a large majority of the Brennans of north Connacht, counties Mayo, Sligo and Roscommon, descend from them. *Ó Braonáin* originated in at least four distinct areas: Kilkenny, east

of Kenmare in Kerry and Lord Oranmore and Browne and the Earls of Altamont in Connacht. The assimilation of the Connacht family into Gaelic life is seen in their inclusion as one of the 'Tribes' of Galway.

In Ulster, where it is more often plain 'Brown', the surname can be an anglicisation of the Scots Gaelic *Mac a' Bhruithin* ('son of the judge') or *Mac Gille Dhuinn* ('son of the brown boy'). The largest concentrations of the name in this province are in counties Derry, Down and Antrim.

BUCKLEY

The common English surname Buckley derives from a number of places of the name, and was used as the anglicisation for the Irish *Ó Buachalla*, derived from *buachaill*, meaning 'boy' or 'herdsman'. In seventeenth-century records, the surname is principally found in Co. Tipperary, but today counties Cork and Kerry have the largest concentrations. Numerically, it is one of the most frequent Irish surnames; almost three-quarters of the Buckleys in the country live in Munster, however. Other, rarer, anglicised versions of the name are Bohilly, Boughla, and Boughil.

One well-known Corkman of the name was Dermot Buckley, one of the last of the eighteenth-century Rapparees, or highwaymen, whose exploits around the Blackwater valley were legendary.

BURKE

Burke, along with its variants Bourke and de Burgh, is now by far the most common Irish name of Norman origin; it is estimated that over 20,000 individuals now bear the surname in Ireland, a figure that probably represents only a fraction of the world-wide total.

The first person of the name to arrive in Ireland was William Fitzadelm de Burgo, a Norman knight from Burgh in Suffolk, who took part in the invasion of 1171 and succeeded Strongbow as Chief Governor. He received the earldom of Ulster, and was granted vast tracts of territory in Connacht. His descendants adopted Gaelic laws and customs more completely than any of the other Norman invaders, and very quickly became one of the most important families in the country. In Connacht, which remained the centre of the family's

BROWNE

Galway, Westmeath and Kerry. Of these the most powerful were the *Ó Braonáin* of Kilkenny, chiefs of Idough in the north of the county. After they lost their land and status to the English, many of them became notorious as leaders of bands of outlaws.

A separate family, the *Ó Branáin*, are the ancestors of many of the Brennans of counties Fermanagh and Monaghan, where the name was also anglicised as Brannan and Branny.

BROWNE

This is one of the most common surnames in the British Isles, and is among the forty commonest in Ireland. It can derive, as a nickname, from the Old English *Brun*, referring to hair, complexion or clothes, or from the Norman name *Le Brun*, similarly meaning 'the Brown'. In the three southern provinces of Munster, Leinster and Connacht, where the name is usually spelt with the final 'e', it is almost invariably of Norman or English origin, and was borne by some of the most important of Norman-Irish and Anglo-Irish families, notably the Earls

BURKE

power, new septs were formed on native Irish lines. William Liath de Burgh, a great-grandson of the original William, was the ancestor of the two most influential clans, the MacWilliam Uachtar of Co. Galway, and the MacWilliam Íochtar of Co. Mayo. Other descendants founded families which created distinct surnames; 'Philbin' derives from *Mac Philbín*, son of Philip (de Burgh); Jennings, now common in Co. Galway, is an anglicisation of *Mac Sheoinín*, son of John (de Burgh); Gibbons, found in Mayo, was originally *Mac Giobúin*, son of Gilbert (de Burgh).

According to legend, the arms of the family originated during the Crusades, when King Richard dipped his finger in the blood of a Saracen slain by one of the de Burghs, drew a cross on the Saracen's golden shield, and presented it to the victor.

BURNS

The surname Burns is Scottish and northern English in origin, and in Ireland is found most frequently in counties Antrim, Down, and Armagh, and in Ulster generally,

The Burns tartan

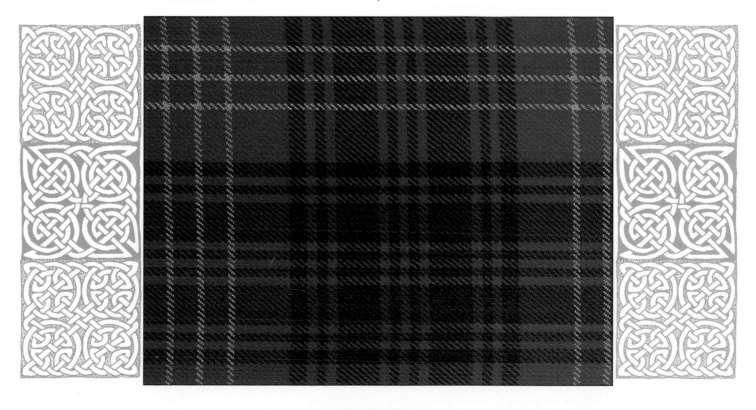

which is home to more than two-thirds of the Irish who bear the name. It comes from the Middle English *burn*, meaning 'a stream', and would have referred to someone who lived close to a river or stream.

The most important source of the name is the Scottish Clan Campbell. The ancestors of the poet Robert Burns moved from Burnhouse near Loch Etive to Forfar, where they became known as the Campbells of Burness. In 1786, Robert and his brother adopted the spelling 'Burns' as a surname, and his subsequent celebrity inspired others to follow his example.

In Ulster, Burns was also used as an anglicisation of the Irish O'Byrne and MacBrin.

BUTLER

The surname Butler, found in both England and Ireland, is Norman in origin, and originally meant 'wine steward', from the same root as modern French *bouteille*, 'bottle'. The name was then extended to denote the chief servant of a household and, in the households of royalty and the most powerful nobility, a high-ranking officer concerned only nominally with the supply of wine.

In Ireland the most prominent Butler family is descended from Theobald Fitzwalter, who was created

BUTLER

Kilkenny Castle, from 1391 until 1936 the chief seat of the Butler earls, dukes and marquesses of Ormond.

BYRNE

CAHILL

'Chief Butler' of Ireland by Henry II in 1177. His descendants became the Earls of Ormond in 1328 and Dukes of Ormond after the restoration of Charles II in 1660. Up to the end of the seventeenth century, the Butlers were one of the most powerful Anglo-Norman dynasties, sharing effective control of Ireland with their great rivals the Fitzgeralds, Earls of Desmond and Earls of Kildare. From the Middle Ages right up to the twentieth century their seat was Kilkenny Castle.

BYRNE

Byrne or O'Byrne, together with its variants Be(i)rne and Byrnes, is one of the ten most frequent surnames in Ireland today. In the original Irish the name is *Ó Broin*, from the personal name *Bran*, meaning 'raven'. It is traced back to King Bran of Leinster, who ruled in the eleventh century.

As a result of the Norman invasion, the O'Byrnes were driven from their original homeland in Co. Kildare into south Co. Wicklow in the early thirteenth century. There they grew in importance over the years, retaining

control of the territory until the early seventeenth century, despite repeated attempts by the English authorities to dislodge them.

Even today, the vast majority of the Irish who bear the name originate in Wicklow or the surrounding counties.

CAHILL

The original Irish from which the name derives is *Ó Cathail*, from the common personal name *Cathal*, sometimes anglicised 'Charles', which may in turn derive from the Old Irish *catu-ualos,* meaning 'strong in battle'.

Families of the name arose separately in different parts of Ireland, in Kerry, Galway, Tipperary and Clare. Originally the Galway family, located in the old diocese of Kilmacduagh near the Clare border, were most prominent, but their position was usurped by the O'Shaughnessys, and they declined. The southern families flourished, and the name is now most common in counties Cork, Kerry and Tipperary, while it is relatively infrequent in its other original homes. The arms illustrated are those of the Munster Cahills.

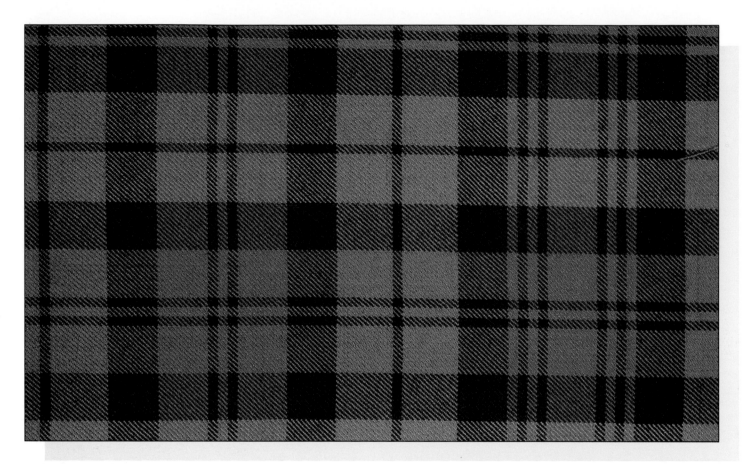

CAMPBELL

Campbell is a Scottish surname, one of the ten most numerous in that country, and one of the thirty most numerous in Ireland, with over two-thirds of those who bear the name living in Ulster. It is particularly common in counties Armagh, Down and Antrim. Originally a nickname, it comes from the Scots Gaelic *cam beul*, meaning 'crooked mouth'.

Clan Campbell was founded by Gillespie Ó Duibhne, who lived in the thirteenth century, and was the first to assume the surname. His descendants included the most famous branch, the Campbells of Argyll, one of whose members was responsible for the massacre of MacDonalds of Glencoe, which led to the famous feud between the two clans.

The vast majority of Irish Campbells are descended from the Scottish family, although in Co. Tyrone the surname may be an anglicisation of the Irish *Mac Cathmhaoil*, from *Cathmhaol*, meaning 'battle-champion'.

Above and below: two variants of the Campbell tartan.

CARROLL

Above: the brass crest of the Carroll arms.

CARROLL

One of the twenty-five most common Irish surnames, Carroll comes, in the vast majority of cases, from the Irish *O Cearbhaill*, from *Cearbhall,* a very popular personal name thought to mean 'fierce in battle'. It is widespread today throughout the three southern provinces of Connacht, Leinster and Munster, reflecting the fact that it arose almost simultaneously as a separate surname in at least six different parts of Ireland.

The most famous of these were the Ely O'Carrolls of *Uíbh Fhailí*, including modern Co. Offaly as well as parts of Tipperary, who derived their name from *Cearball,* King of Ely, one of the leaders of the victorious native Irish army at the battle of Clontarf in 1014. Although their power was much reduced over the centuries in the continuing conflict with the Norman Butlers, they held on to their distinctive Gaelic customs and way of life until the start of the seventeenth century.

CASEY

Casey, O'Casey and MacCasey come from the Irish *cathasach*, meaning 'vigilant in war', a personal name

CASEY

CASSIDY

which was quite common in early Ireland. This, no doubt, accounts for the fact that *Ó Cathasaigh* arose as a separate surname in at least five distinct areas, in counties Cork, Dublin, Fermanagh, Limerick and Mayo, with *Mac Cathasaigh* confined to the Louth/Monaghan area. In medieval times, the Dublin and Fermanagh Caseys were the most prominent, though their power had been broken by the seventeenth century; the name is still common in north Co. Dublin to this day, as it is in Mayo and north Connacht generally. However, most present-day bearers of the surname are to be found in Munster, not only in Cork and Limerick, but also in Kerry and Tipperary.

The arms shown are those of the Co. Limerick sept, part of the great tribe of the *Dál gCais*, who claimed descent from *Cas*, a semi-mythical prehistoric figure. The depiction of the eagle, with its legendary ability to look into the sun without blinking, may be connected to one of the old tribal gods of the *Dál gCais*, *Derctheine*, the fiery-eyed one.

CASSIDY

In Irish *Ó Caiside*, 'descendant of *Caiside*', from *Cas*, meaning 'curly-headed', the surname is inextricably associated with Co. Fermanagh, where the family were

CLANCY

famous for centuries as poets, churchmen, scholars and hereditary physicians to the great Maguire chieftains. In Fermanagh, their original seat was at Ballycassidy, north of Enniskillen. As their healing skills became widely known, many Cassidys were employed by other chiefs, particularly in the north of the country, and the name is now particularly common in counties Donegal, Monaghan and Antrim, as well as in the original homeland of Fermanagh. Although less numerous elsewhere, the name is now also familiar throughout Ireland, with the smallest numbers to be found in Connacht.

CLANCY

The Irish version of the surname is *Mac Fhlannchaidh*, from the personal name *Flannchadh*, which, it is thought, meant 'red warrior'. It originated separately in two different areas, in counties Clare and Leitrim. In the former, where they were a branch of the McNamaras, their eponymous ancestor being *Flannchadh Mac Conmara*, the Clancys formed part of the great *Dál gCais* tribal group, and acted as hereditary lawyers, or 'brehons', to the O'Brien chieftains. Their homeland

was in the barony of Corcomroe in north Clare, and they remained prominent among the Gaelic aristocracy until the final collapse of that institution in the seventeenth century. The Leitrim family of the name were based in the Rosclogher area of the county, around Lough Melvin. Today, the surname is still most common in Leitrim and Clare, with significant numbers also found in the adjacent counties. The best-known bearer of the name in modern times was probably Willie Clancy, a world-famous uilleann piper and folklorist from Co. Clare, who died in 1973.

CLARKE

Clarke is one of the commonest surnames throughout England, Ireland and Scotland, and has the same remote origin in all cases, the Latin *clericus*, originally meaning 'clergyman' and later 'clerk' or 'scholar'. In Irish this became *cléireach*, the root of the surname *Ó Cléireigh*, which was anglicised in two ways, phonetically as 'Cleary', and by translation as 'Clerk' or 'Clarke'. Up to the beginning of this century, the two surnames were still regarded as interchangeable in some areas of the country. By far the largest number of Clarkes (with or without the final 'e') are to be found today in Ulster, a reflection of the great influx of Scottish settlers in the seventeenth century. Even in Ulster, however, without a clear pedigree it is not possible in individual cases to be sure if the origin of the name is English or Irish. Austin Clarke (1896-1974), poet, dramatist and novelist, was one of the most important Irish literary figures of the twentieth century.

CLEARY

Ó Cléirigh, meaning 'grandson of the scribe' is the Irish for both (O) Cle(a)ry and, in many cases in Ireland, Clarke, as outlined above. The surname is of great antiquity, deriving from *Cléireach* of Connacht, born c. 820. The first of his descendants to use his name as part of a fixed hereditary surname was *Tigherneach Ua Cléirigh*, lord of Aidhne in south Co. Galway, whose death is recorded in the year 916. It seems likely that this is the oldest true surname recorded anywhere in Europe. The power of the family in their original Co. Galway

CLEARY

homeland was broken by the thirteenth century, and they scattered throughout the island, with the most prominent branches settling in Derry and Donegal, where they became famous as poets; in Cavan, where many appear to have anglicised the name as 'Clarke', and in the Kilkenny/Waterford/Tipperary region.

COLEMAN

Although Coleman is a common surname in England, where it is occupational, denoting a burner of charcoal, in Ireland the name is almost always of native Irish origin and generally comes from the personal name *Colmán*, a version of the Latin *Columba*, meaning 'dove'. Its popularity as a personal name was due to the two sixth-century Irish missionary saints of the name, in particular St Columban, who founded monasteries in many places throughout central Europe and whose name is the source of many similar European surnames: *Kolman* (Czech), *Kalman*, (Hungarian), *Columbano* (Italian). The original homeland of the Irish *Ó Colmáin* was in the barony of Tireragh in Co. Sligo, and the surname is still quite common in this area. In the other region where the surname is now plentiful, Co. Cork, it

has a different origin, as an anglicisation of the Irish *Ó Clúmháin*, which has also been commonly rendered as 'Clifford'.

COLLINS

Collins is a very common English surname, derived from a diminutive of Nicholas. As with so many such names, in Ireland it may be either of genuinely English origin, or an anglicised version of an original Irish name. Two such Irish names were transformed into Collins: *Ó Coileáin*, originating in Co. Limerick, and *Ó Cuilleáin* of West Cork. The *Ó Coileáin* were forced to migrate from Limerick to the home territory of the *Ó Cúilleáin* in the thirteenth century, so that it is now virtually impossible to distinguish between the two originals. The name is extremely numerous in Cork and Limerick, and indeed throughout the southern half of the country.

The arms of Ballinasloe, at the centre of the area where the *Ó Connalláin* originated.

CONLON

Conlon and its associated variants (O')Conlan and Connellan, are anglicised versions of a number of Irish names. *Ó'Connalláin*, from a diminutive of the personal name *Conall*, 'strong as a wolf', originated in counties Galway and Roscommon. *Ó Coinghiolláin*, whose derivation is unclear, arose in Co. Sligo. The third of the Irish originals, *Ó Caoindealbháin*, comes from *caoin*, 'fair' or 'comely' and *dealbh*, meaning 'form', and is principally associated with the midlands and Co. Meath. This last

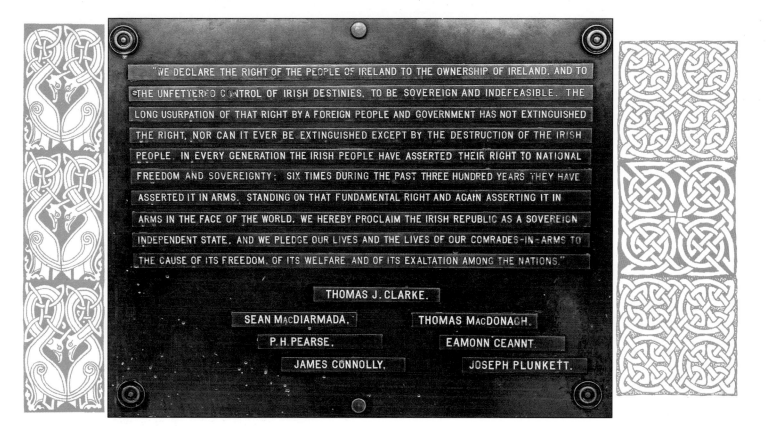

"WE DECLARE THE RIGHT OF THE PEOPLE OF IRELAND TO THE OWNERSHIP OF IRELAND, AND TO THE UNFETTERED CONTROL OF IRISH DESTINIES, TO BE SOVEREIGN AND INDEFEASIBLE. THE LONG USURPATION OF THAT RIGHT BY A FOREIGN PEOPLE AND GOVERNMENT HAS NOT EXTINGUISHED THE RIGHT, NOR CAN IT EVER BE EXTINGUISHED EXCEPT BY THE DESTRUCTION OF THE IRISH PEOPLE. IN EVERY GENERATION THE IRISH PEOPLE HAVE ASSERTED THEIR RIGHT TO NATIONAL FREEDOM AND SOVEREIGNTY; SIX TIMES DURING THE PAST THREE HUNDRED YEARS THEY HAVE ASSERTED IT IN ARMS. STANDING ON THAT FUNDAMENTAL RIGHT AND AGAIN ASSERTING IT IN ARMS IN THE FACE OF THE WORLD. WE HEREBY PROCLAIM THE IRISH REPUBLIC AS A SOVEREIGN INDEPENDENT STATE, AND WE PLEDGE OUR LIVES AND THE LIVES OF OUR COMRADES-IN-ARMS TO THE CAUSE OF ITS FREEDOM, OF ITS WELFARE AND OF ITS EXALTATION AMONG THE NATIONS."

THOMAS J. CLARKE.

SEAN MacDIARMADA.   THOMAS MacDONAGH.

P. H. PEARSE,   EAMONN CEANNT.

JAMES CONNOLLY,   JOSEPH PLUNKETT.

Above: part of the 1916 Proclamation of Independence. James Connolly, one of the signatories, was the founder of modern Irish socialism. Left: the arms of the Connolly family.

name was also anglicised 'Quinlan' or, in Munster, 'Quinlivan'. The most common anglicisation, 'Conlon', is now distributed throughout Ireland, with particular concentrations in the original homelands of north Connacht and the midlands.

CONNOLLY

Again, a number of original Irish names have been anglicised as 'Connolly.' The *Ó Conghalaigh*, from *conghal*, 'as fierce as a wolf', were based in Connacht, where the English version is now often spelt 'Connelly'. The name arose as *Ó Coingheallaigh* in West Cork, while Ulster Connollys derive from both the *Ó Conghalaigh* of Fermanagh, who gave their name to Derrygonnelly, 'Connolly's oakwood', and the Monaghan Connollys, for whom a number of separate origins are suggested, as a branch of the southern *Uí Néill*, or as a branch of the

Begun in 1722 for William Conolly [*sic*], Speaker of the Irish House of Commons, Castletown House, Co. Kildare is the finest Georgian house in Ireland.

MacMahons. Whatever their origin, the Monaghan family have been the most prominent of the Connollys, recorded as having 'Chiefs of the Name' up to the seventeenth century, and producing, among others, Speaker William Conolly [*sic*], reputedly the richest man in eighteenth-century Ireland, and James Connolly, labour leader, socialist writer, and signatory of the 1916 Proclamation of Independence. The arms illustrated are those of the family of William Conolly [*sic*].

CONWAY

In Ireland Conway may be of Welsh or Irish origin. In the former case it derives from the fortified town of *Conwy*, from the river of the same name, which term is thought to mean 'reedy'. Descendants of settlers of the name are to found in counties Kerry and Antrim, and elsewhere. The Irish origins of the name are manifold: it is the

The arms of Westport, Co. Mayo, the part of Ireland where the name Conway is today most numerous.

anglicised version of at least four separate names, including, in Co. Sligo, *Ó Conbhuidhe*, ('yellow hound'), also anglicised 'Conboy'; in Mayo *Ó Connmhacháin*, sometimes also given as 'Convey'; in Munster *Mac Connmháigh*, from *condmhach*, meaning 'head-smashing', also anglicised 'Conoo', and in Derry/Tyrone *Mac Conmídhe* ('Hound of Meath'), which has also

been rendered as 'MacConomy', 'Conomy' etc. The surname is now numerous throughout Ireland, with perhaps the largest single concentration in Co. Mayo.

The Arms of Cashel, in the heart of an area where many Corcorans still live today.

CORCORAN

The English version may derive from a number of Irish originals: *Ó Corcráin*, *Mac Corcráin*, *Ó Corcáin*, and *Ó Corcra*, all stemming originally from *corcair*, meaning 'purple'. The name has also been anglicised 'Corkery' and 'Corkin'. It arose separately in different locations, in the O'Carroll territory encompassing parts of Offaly and Tipperary, and in Co. Fermanagh. The name is now rare in Fermanagh, and it seems likely that the many Corcorans found in Mayo and Sligo are part of this group. Further south the name is also common now in Cork and Kerry as well as in Tipperary.

COSTELLO

The origin of the surname Costello provides a perfect illustration of the way the native Irish absorbed the invading Normans. Soon after the invasion, the de Angulo family, also known as 'Nangle', settled in Connacht, where they rapidly became powerful. After only three generations, they had begun to give themselves a surname formed in the Irish manner, with the clan taking Jocelyn de Angulo as their eponymous forebear. Jocelyn was rendered *Goisdealbh* in Irish, and the surname adopted was *Mac Goisdealbhaigh*, later given

COSTELLO

the phonetic English equivalent 'Costello'. Their power continued up to the seventeenth century, centred in east Mayo, where they gave their name to the barony of Costello. Today the surname is widely spread throughout Ireland, with the largest concentrations still in the historic homeland of Connacht.

COUGHLAN

Two original Irish versions of Coughlan (and its variants (O') Coghlan, Coglin and Cohalan) exist, *Ó Cochláin* and *Mac Cochláin*, both derived from *cochall*, meaning 'cloak' or 'hood'. The *Mac Cochláin* were part of the great tribal grouping of the *Dál gCais*, claiming descent from the semi-mythical *Cas*, which also produced O'Briens and the McNamaras. Their territory was in the

COUGHLAN

present Co. Offaly, where they remained prominent up to the eighteenth century. Co. Cork was the homeland of the *Ó Cochláin*, where the name has long been associated with the baronies of East and West Carbury, and Barrymore. Interestingly, the surname tends to be pronounced differently in different areas of Co. Cork, as 'Cocklin' in the west and 'Cawlin' in the east.

CRAIG

Craig is Scottish in origin, describing a person who lived near a steep or sheer rock, from the Scots Gaelic *creag*.

It was very common near Edinburgh and the Lowlands in the fifteenth and sixteenth centuries, and was brought to Ulster by seventeenth-century Scottish settlers. In Ireland, it is still almost exclusive to Ulster, where it is now one of the most numerous surnames, being particularly frequent in Co. Antrim, with large numbers also to be found in counties Derry and Tyrone. The most famous Irish bearer of the name, who organised the Ulster Volunteer Force against Home Rule after 1912, was prime minister of Northern Ireland from its creation in 1921 until his death in 1940. He was created Viscount Craigavon in 1927, and the new town of Craigavon in Co. Armagh is named after him.

The Craig tartan

The arms of Cork, associated throughout history
with the Cronins.

CRONIN

The surname in Irish is *Ó Cróinín*, from a diminutive of *crón*, meaning 'yellow' or 'swarthy'. A more accurate rendition of the original pronunciation would be 'Croneen', and this survives in placenames embodying the name Cooscronin ('Cronin's hollow') and Liscroneen ('Cronin's fort') in west Cork, and Ballycroneen in Imokilly barony in east Cork. As the placenames imply, the origin of the family lies in Cork, in particular in the west of the county, where they were originally part of

the *Corca Laoighdhe*. In the Gaelic genealogies of this tribal grouping, the Cronins are recorded as hereditary owners of territory to the west of present-day Clonakilty.

CROWLEY

CROWLEY

In form Crowley is English, a habitation name from an Old English term meaning 'wood of the crows', and no doubt some of those in Ireland bearing the name derive from English stock. However, the vast majority are of Gaelic Irish extraction, with Crowley an anglicisation of *Ó Cruadhlaoich*, from *cruadh* and *laoch*, meaning 'hardy' and 'warrior'. The *Cruadhlaoch* from whom the family take their name was in fact one of the MacDermots of Moylurg in Connacht, who lived in the mid-11th century. Some time later, probably in the thirteenth century, some members of the family migrated from Connacht to Co. Cork, and their descendants prospered and multiplied while the original western branch of the family declined. The vast majority of Irish Crowleys today are connected to the Cork branch, and that county is still home to most of them. Up to the seventeenth century they remained powerful, particularly in the Carbery region of the county, and acquired a reputation as formidable soldiers, literally living up to their name.

CULLEN

The surname Cullen may be of Norman or Gaelic origin. The Norman name has been derived both from the city of Cologne in Germany, and from Colwyn in Wales. In Ireland this Norman family was prominent principally in Co. Wexford, where their seat was at Cullenstown castle in Bannow parish. Much more numerous in modern times, however, are descendants of the *Ó Cuilinn*, a name taken from *cuileann*, meaning 'holly-tree'. The name originated in southeast Leinster, and this area has remained their stronghold, with the majority to be found even today in counties Wicklow and Wexford. The most famous individual of the name was Paul Cullen (1803-78), Cardinal and Archbishop of Dublin, who presided over, and guided, the revival of the power of the Catholic Church in nineteenth-century Ireland.

CUNNINGHAM

In form, Cunningham is originally Scottish, taken from the place of the same name near Kilmarnock in Ayrshire. This name was originally *Cuinneagán*, from the Scots Gaelic *cuinneag*, meaning 'milk-pail', and was given its present form through the mistake of a twelfth-century English scribe, who transcribed the ending as '-ham', a purely English suffix meaning 'village'. Many Scottish Cunninghams came to Ireland in the seventeenth-century Plantation of Ulster, and their descendants now form the bulk of those bearing the name in that province, where it is most numerous. As well as these, however, many of native Gaelic stock also adopted Cunningham as the anglicised version of their names. Among these were the *Mac Cuinneagáin* (MacCunnigan) of Co. Donegal, the *Ó Cuineagáin* or *Ó Cuineacháin* (Kennigan/Kinahan) of Co. Antrim, the *Ó Connacháin* (Conaghan) of counties Tyrone and Derry, the *Mac Donnegáin* (Donegan) of Co. Down and the *Ó Connagáin* (Conagan) of Co. Armagh. The most numerous, however, were the *Ó Connagáin* and *Mac Cuinneagáin* of Connacht, where the surname remains

CULLEN

most common outside Ulster. The Scottish influx, together with the large number of Irish originals which Cunningham came to represent, have made it common and widespread throughout Ireland.

CURRAN

Curran, together with its many variants (O')Curren, Corhen, Currane, Curreen etc. may come from the Irish *Ó Corraidhín*, or *Ó Corráin*, both deriving from *corradh*, meaning 'spear'. The former version arose in Co. Donegal, where it still remains very numerous, while the latter was the name of several independent septs living in south Leinster/Waterford, Kerry, Galway and Leitrim. Today, the heaviest concentration of the name is found in Ulster, with the smallest number in Connacht, but the

name is numerous and widespread throughout Ireland. Its most famous bearers were John Philpot Curran (1750-1817), the barrister and nationalist, and his daughter Sarah, who was secretly engaged to Robert Emmett. Thomas Moore's song *She is Far From the Land* was inspired by her story.

DALY

DALY

The surname (O) Daly (and its variants Daily, Daley etc.) is *Ó Dálaigh* in Irish, deriving from *Dálach* meaning 'one who is present at assemblies'; the root word is *Dáil*, now the official title of the parliament of the Republic of Ireland. A connection is possible between the meaning of the name and the long tradition of scholarship and poetic achievement associated with those who bear it, since the *ollamh* of Gaelic Ireland had a place of honour at the tribal *dáil* as a man of learning and a poet. The medieval genealogists located their homeland in the present Co. Westmeath, and they spread throughout the country by acting as *ollamhs* to the most prominent families. From a very early date families of the name were also prominent in Co. Cork, and especially in the area around the peninsula of Muintervarra, or Sheep's Head, in west Cork. The likeliest

explanation is that the name had a separate origin in the south. Even so, the O'Dalys of Desmond had an equally strong association with poetry and learning: so potent were the poems of Aonghas Ó Dálaigh of Ballyroon that he was murdered by one of the victims of his satires. The name is now common throughout Ireland, with the greatest concentrations in the south and west, and in Co. Westmeath.

The arms of Portlaoise, in the original territory of the *Ó Dúbhshláine*.

DELANEY

In its form, Delaney is a Norman name, from *De l'aunaie*, meaning 'from the alder grove', and doubtless some of those bearing the name in Ireland are of Norman stock. However, in the vast majority of cases it was adopted as the anglicised form of the original Irish *Ó Dúbhshláine*, from *dubh*, meaning 'black', and *slán*, meaning 'defiance'. The original territory of the *Ó Dúbhshláine* was at the foot of the Slieve Bloom mountains in Co. Laois. From there they spread also in neighbouring Co. Kilkenny, and the surname is still strongly associated with these two counties. The most famous historical bearer of the surname was Patrick Delaney (1685/6-1768), Church of Ireland clergyman, renowned preacher and close friend of Jonathan Swift, of whom he wrote a celebrated 'Defence'.

DEMPSEY

In the original Irish Dempsey is *Ó Díomasaigh*, from *díomasach*, meaning 'proud'. The name was also

DEMPSEY

DILLON

occasionally anglicised 'Proudman'. The *Ó Díomasaigh* originated in the territory of Clanmalier, on the borders of what are now counties Laois and Offaly, and remained powerful in the area until the seventeenth century. James I recognised the strength of the family by granting the title 'Viscount Clanmalier' to Terence Dempsey. The loyalty of the family to the crown was short-lived, however, and the Williamite wars later in the century destroyed their power and scattered them. The surname is now found throughout the country. In Ulster, Dempsey is common in Co. Antrim, where it may be a version of 'Dempster', a Scottish name meaning 'judge', or possibly an anglicisation of *Mac Díomasaigh*, also sometimes rendered as 'McGimpsey'.

DILLON

In Ireland Dillon may be of Gaelic or Norman origin, the former from *Ó Duilleáin*, possibly from *dall*, meaning 'blind', the latter from *de Leon*, from the place of the same name in Brittany. This, of course, accounts for the lion in the family arms. The Norman family have been prominent in Ireland since the arrival of their ancestor Sir Henry de Leon in 1185. He was granted vast estates in counties Longford and Westmeath, and his descendants retained their power up to modern times, with Co. Westmeath becoming known simply as 'Dillon's Country'. Another branch of the family settled in Co. Mayo, where they are still well known today. After the Williamite wars of the seventeenth century, a number of members of the family served in Continental armies. The best-known Irish regiment in the French army was 'Dillon's Regiment', many members of which made their way to America to fight against the British in the War of Independence.

DOHERTY

Doherty and its many variants – (O')Dogherty, Docherty, Dougharty etc., comes from the Irish *Ó Dochartaigh*, from *dochartach*, meaning 'unlucky' or 'hurtful'. The original *Dochartach,* from whom the clan descend, lived in the tenth century and has traditionally been claimed as twelfth in lineal descent from Conall

DOHERTY

DOLAN

In Irish the surname is *Ó Dúbhshláin*, from *dubh*, meaning 'black' and *slán*, meaning 'challenge' or 'defiance'. Other anglicised versions include 'Doolan' and 'Dowling'. It first arose as part of the *Uí Máine* tribal grouping in south Roscommon and east Galway, and from there spread to the northeast into counties Leitrim, Cavan and Fermanagh. It remains numerous in all five counties today, and is particularly common in Co. Cavan. In places it is also given as an anglicisation of *Ó Doibhilin*, probably derived from *dobhail*, meaning 'unlucky', and more usually rendered into English as 'Devlin'. Many of the Dolans of Co. Sligo are of this stock.

DONNELLY

Donnelly is *Ó Donnáile* in Irish, from Donnáil, a personal name made up of *donn*, meaning 'brown' and *gal*, meaning 'bravery'. The original ancestor was Donnáil O Neill, who died in 876, and was himself a descendant of

DONNELLY

Gulbain, son of Niall of the Nine Hostages, the fifth-century monarch supposedly responsible for kidnapping St Patrick to Ireland, and progenitor of the great tribal grouping of the *Uí Néill*. Conall gave his name to the territory he conquered, *Tír Chónaill*, the Irish for Donegal, and to the subgroup of the *Uí Néill*, the *Cinéal Chonaill*, the race of Conall, the collective name for the many families which claim descent from him, such as the Gallaghers and the O'Donnells as well as the Dohertys. The original homeland of the O'Dohertys was in the barony of Raphoe in Co. Donegal, with the chief seat at Ardmire in the parish of Kilteevoge. They remained powerful chiefs in the area for five hundred years, until the defeat and execution of Sir Cahir O'Doherty at the start of the seventeenth century.

DORAN

Eoghan, son of Niall of the Nine Hostages, the fifth-century king who supposedly kidnapped St. Patrick to Ireland. Their territory was first in Co. Donegal, but they later moved eastwards into Co. Tyrone, where the centre of their power was at Ballydonnelly. Many of the family were hereditary bards, but their chief historical fame is as soldiers, especially in the wars of the seventeenth century. One modern bearer of the name who combined both traditional roles was Charles Donnelly (1910-37), poet and republican, who was killed fighting with the International Brigade in the Spanish Civil War.

DORAN

Doran is in Irish *Ó Deoráin*, a contracted form of *Ó Deoradháin*, from *deoradh*, meaning 'exile' or 'pilgrim'. The surname has also been anglicised as 'Dorrian', principally in the northern counties of Armagh and Down, where a branch was established in early times.

DOWD

DOWLING

The major fame of the family, however, was in Leinster, where for centuries they were hereditary judges and lawyers ('brehons') to the rulers of the ancient territory of *Uí Cinnsealaigh*, the MacMurroughs. This territory took in all of the present Co. Wexford as well as adjoining parts of south Wicklow and Carlow, and the Dorans are still most numerous in this area today, with the placename 'Doransland' in Wexford providing evidence of their long association with the area. In modern times, Dorans have been famous as Wexford sportsmen, with families from Enniscorthy, Monamolin and Gorey prominent in football, hurling and cycling.

DOWD

At the end of the nineteenth century, the vast majority of bearers of this surname, by a proportion of four to one, were 'Dowd' rather than 'O'Dowd'. Since then, a large-scale resumption of the 'O' has reversed the proportions, with 'O'Dowd' now by far the most popular. The original Irish name was *Ó Dubhda*, from *dubh*, meaning 'black'. In the traditional genealogies, the family is one of the *Uí Fiachrach*, a large tribal grouping tracing

its origin back to Fiachra, brother of Niall of the Nine Hostages, the fifth-century monarch supposedly responsible for kidnapping St Patrick to Ireland. The O'Dowds were the most powerful in this group, and for centuries their territory included large parts of northwest Mayo and west Sligo; the name is still numerous in the area today. The surname also appears to have arisen separately in two other areas of the country: in Munster, where the anglicisations 'Doody' and 'Duddy' are quite frequent in the Kerry area, and in Derry, where the anglicisation is almost invariably 'Duddy'.

DOWLING

Although it may sometimes appear as a variant of 'Dolan', in most cases Dowling has a separate origin. In form the name is English, derived from the Old English *dol*, meaning 'dull' or 'stupid', but in Ireland it is generally an anglicisation of the Irish *Ó Dúnlaing*. The original territory of the *Ó Dúnlaing* was in the west of the present Co. Laois, along the banks of the river Barrow, which was known as *Fearrann ua nDúnlaing*, 'O'Dowling's country'. The leading members of the family were transplanted to Tarbert in Co. Kerry in 1609, along with other leaders of the 'Seven Septs of Laois', but the surname remained numerous in its original homeland, and spread south and west into Carlow, Kilkenny, Wicklow and Dublin, where it is now very common. As a first name *Dúnlang* was popular in early medieval times in Leinster, where it was also anglicised as 'Dudley'.

DOYLE

This name, one of the most common in Ireland, derives from the Irish *Ó Dubhghaill*, from *dubh*, 'dark', and *gall*, 'foreigner', a descriptive formula first used to describe the invading Vikings, and in particular to distinguish the darker-haired Danes from fair-haired Norwegians. The common Scottish names 'Dougall' and 'MacDougall' come from the same source, and reflect the original pronunciation more accurately. In Ulster and Roscommon, these names now exist as 'McDowell' and 'Dowell', carried by the descendants of immigrant Scottish gallowglasses, or mercenaries. The strongest association of Doyle, however, is with southeast Leinster, counties Wexford, Wicklow and Carlow in particular, though the name is now found everywhere in Ireland. The stag portrayed in the arms is regarded as a symbol of permanence and endurance, a theme reflected also in one of the family mottoes *Bhí mé beich mé*, 'I was and I will be'.

DRISCOLL

In 1890, over 90 per cent of those bearing the name recorded themselves as 'Driscoll'; today, in a remarkable reversal of the nineteenth-century trend, virtually all are called 'O'Driscoll'. The surname comes from the Irish *O hEidirsceoil*, from *eidirsceol*, meaning 'go-between' or 'bearer of news'. The original *Eidirsceol* from whom the family descend was born in the early tenth century, and since then they have been strongly associated with west Cork, in particular the area around Baltimore and Skibbereen, where they remained powerful up to the seventeenth century. They were part of the *Corca Laoighde* tribal grouping, descended from the *Érainn* or *Fir Bolg*, Celts who were settled in Ireland well before the arrival of the Gaels, and retained

DOYLE

DRISCOLL

a distinct identity despite the dominance of the victorious newcomers. Their arms reflect the family's traditional prowess as seafarers, developed during their long lordship of the seacoast around Baltimore.

DUFFY

In Irish the surname is *Ó Dubhthaigh*, from *dubhthach*, meaning 'the dark one'. Several different families of the name arose separately in different places, the most important being in Donegal, Roscommon and Monaghan. In Donegal the family were centred on the parish of Templecrone, where they remained powerful churchmen for almost eight hundred years. The Roscommon family, too, had a long association with the church, producing a succession of distinguished abbots and bishops. The area around Lissonuffy in the northeast of the county, which is named after them, was the centre of their influence. From this source the name is now common in north Connacht. The Monaghan O'Duffys were rulers of the area around Clontibret. They also contributed a great deal to the church, with a huge number of parish clergy of the name. They flourished through the centuries, and Duffy is now the single most common name in Co. Monaghan.

Second-hand bookshops abound in Dublin. Duffy's in Leinster Row is one of the largest.

DUGGAN

The Irish *Ó Dubhagáin* is anglicised principally as 'Duggan', but may also be found as 'Dugan' or 'Doogan', the latter representing a more accurate rendition of the Irish pronunciation. The principal family of the name had their territory near the modern town of Fermoy in north Cork, and were part of the *Fir Máighe* tribal grouping which gave its name to the town. Along with

DUGGAN

the other *Fir Máighe* families they lost their power when the Normans conquered the territory in the twelfth and thirteenth centuries. The family name is found in the parish and townland of Caherduggan in that area. Another sept of the same name is famous in the *Uí Máine* area of east Galway/south Roscommon principally because it produced John O'Dugan (died 1372), chief poet of the O'Kellys, and co-author of the *Topographical Poems*, a long, detailed description of Ireland in the twelfth century. The arms of the family appear to derive from a pun on some of the elements of the name *dubh*, meaning 'dark' and *án*, meaning 'light'.

DUNNE

DWYER

DUNNE

Although 'Dunn' is also an English surname, from the Old English *dunn*, 'dark-coloured', the vast majority of those bearing the name in Ireland descend from the *Ó Doinn*, from *donn*, used to describe someone who was swarthy or brown-haired. The *Ó Doinn* first came to prominence as lords of the area around Tinnehinch in the north of the modern Co. Laois, and were known as Lords of Iregan up to the seventeenth century. At that time the surname was generally anglicised as 'O'Doyne'. Today the name is still extremely common in that part of Ireland, though it is now also widespread elsewhere. Perhaps because of the stronger English influence, in Ulster the name is generally spelt 'Dunn', while it is almost invariably 'Dunne' in other parts.

DWYER

In Irish the surname is *Ó Duibhir* or *Ó Dubhuidhir*, made up of *dubh*, meaning 'dark' and *odhar*, meaning 'tawny' or 'sallow'. The resumption of the 'O' prefix has now made 'O'Dwyer' much the most common version. Their original homeland was in the mountains of west Tipperary, where they held power and resisted the encroachments of the English down to modern times. The surname is still extremely common in this area, but Dwyers and O'Dwyers have now also spread into the neighbouring counties of Limerick, Cork and Kilkenny. The most famous bearer of the name in modern times was Michael Dwyer, who took part in the 1798 Rising against the English, and continued his resistance up to 1803. He was transported to New South Wales in Australia, and became High Constable of Sydney, where he died in 1826.

EGAN

Egan in Irish is *Mac Aodhagáin*, from a diminutive of the personal name *Aodh*, meaning 'fire', which was anglicised 'Hugh' for some strange reason. As well as Egan, *Aodh* is also the root of many other common Irish surnames, including O'Higgins, O'Hea, Hayes, McHugh, McCoy etc. The *MacAodhagáin* originated in the *Uí Máine* territory of south Roscommon/east Galway, where they were hereditary lawyers and judges to the ruling families. Over the centuries, however, they became dispersed southwards, settling mainly in north Munster and east Leinster. As well as Connacht, their original homeland, they are now most numerous in Leinster, though the

FAHY

EGAN

surname is now also relatively widespread throughout Ireland. In both Connacht and Leinster the surname has also sometimes been anglicised as 'Keegan'.

FAHY

Fahy in Irish is *Ó Fathaigh*, probably from *fothadh* meaning 'base' or 'foundation'. Another, rarer, English version of the name is 'Vahey'. Strangely, it has also been anglicised as 'Green' because of a mistaken association with *faithce*, meaning 'lawn'. The name still has a very strong association with Co. Galway, where the historic homeland was situated. The area of the family's power was around the modern town of Loughrea in the south of the county, and the surname is still most plentiful in this area, despite the upheavals and migrations which have spread the name quite widely throughout Ireland. The best-known bearer of the name was Francis Arthur Fahy (1854-1935), songwriter and literary man, who paved the way for the Irish Literary Revival through his lifelong involvement with the Gaelic League and the London Irish Literary Society.

FARRELL

As both (O')Farrell and (O')Ferrall, this name in Irish is *Fearghail*, from the personal name *Fearghal*, made up of *fear*, 'man', and *gal*, 'valour'. The original *Fearghal* or Fergal from whom the family claim descent was killed

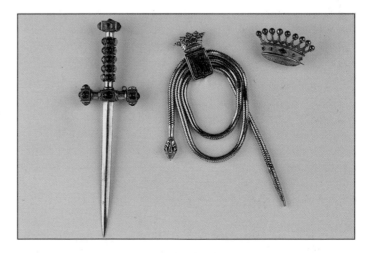

The jewelled neck ornaments and dagger of the O'Farrells of Annally, in the State Heraldic Museum.

FARRELL

FINNEGAN

at Clontarf in 1014. His great grandfather Angall gave his name to the territory they possessed, Annally in Co. Longford. The present name of both the county and the town derives from the family, the full name in Irish being *Longphuirt Uí Fhearghaíll*, O'Farrell's Fortress. They ruled this area for almost seven centuries, down to the final catastrophes of the seventeenth century, after which many members of the family fought with distinction in the armies of continental Europe. Today the surname is one of the most common in Ireland, with a wide distribution throughout the country, though the largest concentration remains in the historical homeland of Longford and the surrounding areas. The most famous modern Irish bearer of the name was Michael Farrell (1899-1962), whose novel *Thy Tears Might Cease* achieved international recognition in the 1960s.

FERGUSON

The surname is common in Scotland, and in Ireland is almost entirely confined to Ulster because of the Scottish connection. It is particularly numerous in counties Antrim, Derry, Fermanagh and Down. Most Irish Fergusons claim descent from Fergus, prince of Galloway, who died in 1161, whose descendants included the Fergusons of Craigdarrach in Dumfriesshire, and of Atholl and Dunfallandy in Perthshire. The connection remains somewhat speculative, since the root of the name, the personal name Fergus, was common and widespread in medieval Scotland, and almost certainly gave rise to a large number of different families bearing the surname. Sir Samuel Ferguson (1810-86) was a precursor of the Irish Literary Revival, publishing many

translations from Irish and versions of Irish myths, as well as contributing greatly to the scientific study of early Irish antiquities.

Cavan and Monaghan. It is now also common throughout Ireland, with the exception of the southern province of Munster.

FINNEGAN

In Irish the surname is *Ó Fionnagáin*, from *Fionnagán*, a diminutive of the popular personal name *Fionn*, meaning 'fairhaired'. It arose separately in two areas, on the borders of the present north Roscommon and north-east Galway, between the modern towns of Dunmore and Castlerea, and in the territory taking in parts of the present counties of Monaghan, Cavan and Louth. Descendants of the Connacht family are still to be found in the ancestral homeland, but the majority of modern Finnegans are descended from the Ulster family, and the name remains particularly numerous in counties

FITZGERALD

Fitzgerald is a Norman name, made up of *Fi(t)z*, Norman French for 'son of', and Gerald, a personal name of Germanic origin from *geri*, 'spear' and *wald*, 'rule'. The family trace their origin to Walter FitzOther, keeper of Windsor forest in the late eleventh century, whose son Gerald was constable of Pembroke Castle in Wales.

The ruins of the Franciscan friary at Askeaton, Co. Limerick, founded in the fourteenth century by Gerald Fitzgerald, 4th Earl of Desmond, and restored in the fifteenth century by his successor James, the 6th Earl.

Gerald's son Walter accompanied Strongbow in the invasion of Ireland, and adopted the surname Fitzgerald. Over the following eight centuries the family became one of the most powerful and numerous in Ireland. The head of the main branch, the Duke of Leinster, known historically as the Earl of Kildare, is the foremost peer of Ireland. The power of the Munster branch, the Earls of Desmond, was severely disrupted in the wars of the sixteenth century, but gave rise to three hereditary titles, in existence since at least 1333, which still survive: the Knight of Kerry, the Knight of Glin, and the White Knight, now a Fitzgibbon. The surname is now common, but remains concentrated in the ancient homeland of the Earls of Desmond, counties Cork, Limerick and Kerry.

FITZPATRICK

Despite its Norman appearance, 'Fitz-' being Norman French for 'son of', in the vast majority of cases Fitzpatrick is an anglicisation of the Irish *Mac Giolla Phádraig*, meaning 'son of the servant of (St) Patrick'. Similarly to other surnames containing *Giolla*, it has also been anglicised as 'Kilpatrick' and, more rarely, 'Gilpatrick', principally in Ulster, where it is most common in counties Fermanagh and Monaghan. The original *Giolla Phádraig* from whom the surname is taken was the tenth-century ruler of the ancient kingdom of Upper Ossory, including parts of the present counties of Laois and Kilkenny. The surname was anglicised to Fitzpatrick in the early sixteenth century, when the chief of the family accepted the title of Lord Baron of Upper Ossory from Henry VIII. Partly due to this, they managed to retain possession of a large portion of their original lands right up to the nineteenth century. Although the surname is now common and widespread throughout Ireland, the largest concentration is still to be found in Co. Laois, part of their original homeland.

FLAHERTY

In Irish Flaherty and O'Flaherty are *Ó Flaithbheartach*, from *flaitheamh*, meaning 'prince' or 'ruler', and *beartach*, meaning 'acting' or 'behaving'. Although the

FITZGERALD FITZPATRICK

FLAHERTY

FLANAGAN

literal translation is 'one who behaves like a prince', a more accurate rendition would be 'hospitable' or 'generous'. The family's original territory included the whole of the west of the modern Co. Galway, including Connemara and the Aran Islands, whence the title of their chief, Lord of Iar-Chonnacht and of Moycullen. They occupied and controlled this area from the thirteenth century on, and survived as a power in the area down to the eighteenth century. Although the name is now common and widespread, the largest numbers are still to be found in Co. Galway.

FLANAGAN

In Irish the surname is *Ó Flannagáin*, a diminutive of *flann*, a personal name which was very popular in early Ireland, and means 'red' or 'ruddy'. Perhaps because of this popularity, the surname arose separately in a number of distinct locations, including counties Roscommon, Fermanagh, Monaghan and Offaly. Of these, the most important families historically were those of Roscommon and Fermanagh. In the former location they were long associated with the royal O'Connors, traditionally deriving from the same stock, and supplying stewards to the royal household. In Fermanagh they were rulers of a large territory covering the west of Lower Lough Erne, and based at Ballyflanagan, now the townland of Aghamore in Magheraboy parish. Today the surname is found widely distributed throughout Ireland, though the largest concentration remains in the areas of their original homelands, southwest Ulster and north Connacht.

The arms of the family display the royal oak, symbol of the O'Connors, proclaiming their long association with this family, though the tree does not cover the whole shield, a significant difference.

FLEMING

'Fleming' is an ethnic name simply meaning 'an inhabitant of Flanders'. It is a common surname in Britain, reflecting the importance of the wool trade between England and the Netherlands in the Middle Ages, when many Flemish weavers and dyers settled in England, Wales and southern Scotland. It arrived in Ireland in two ways: following the Norman invasion,

FLEMING

FLYNN

expected, this popularity led to the surname coming into being independently in several different parts of the country, including Clare, Cork, Kerry, Mayo, Roscommon, Cavan, Antrim and Monaghan. The most historically important of these were the families originating in Cork and Roscommon, with the former ruling over a territory in Muskerry between Ballyvourney and Blarney, and the latter centred on the area of north Roscommon around the modern town of Castlerea. In Co. Antrim the Irish version of the name was *Ó Fhloinn*, with the initial 'F' silent, so that the anglicised version became 'O'Lynn', or simply 'Lynn'. The O'Lynns ruled over the lands between Lough Neagh and the Irish Sea in south Antrim. (O')Flynn is now numerous throughout Ireland, though significant concentrations are still to be found in north Connacht and the Cork/Waterford areas, roughly corresponding to the original homelands.

when families of the name became prominent in the areas around Dublin; and through the Plantation of Ulster in the seventeenth century, when many Scottish bearers of the name arrived. Today, although widespread elsewhere, the surname is most numerous in Ulster, particularly in counties Antrim and Derry, but the most historically important Fleming family was one of the earlier southern arrivals, a family that held large tracts of land in counties Meath and Louth down to the seventeenth century, and acquired the title 'Lords of Slane'.

FLYNN

In Irish the name is *Ó Floinn*, from the adjective *flann*, meaning 'reddish' or 'ruddy', which was extremely popular as a personal name in early Ireland. As might be

FOLEY

The original Irish for the surname is *Ó Foghladha*, from *foghlaidh*, meaning 'pirate' or 'marauder'. It originated in Co. Waterford, and from there spread to the nearby

counties of Cork and Kerry. These are the three locations in which it is still most numerous, though it is now common throughout the southern half of the country. The best known modern Irish bearer of the name, Donal Foley (1922-81), journalist and humorist, came from the original homeland of Co. Waterford. The current Speaker of the U.S. House of Representatives is Congressman Tom Foley.

In places in Ulster the surname MacSharry (*Mac Searraigh*) was sometimes mistranslated as 'Foley' or 'Foaley', because of a mistaken belief that it was derived from *searrach*, meaning 'foal'.

FORD

In form, this is a common English name for someone who lived near a ford. In Ireland, where it is more often 'Forde', it may indicate English ancestry, since many English of the name settled in Ireland. However, in the majority of cases it is a native Irish name, an anglicisation

The desolate beauty of Glenmore Lake in Co. Kerry, now the stronghold of the Foleys.

of at least three Irish distinct originals: *Mac Giolla na Naomh*, meaning 'son of the devotee of the saints', also anglicised as 'Gildernew'; *Mac Conshnámha*, from *conshnámh*, meaning 'swimming dog', also anglicised 'Kinneavy'; and *Ó Fuaráin*, from *fuar*, meaning 'cold', and also anglicised as 'Foran'. Clearly, the English clerks transcribing Irish names had scant knowledge of the language they were hearing. *Mac Conshnámha* originated in north Connacht, where the sept were chiefs in the area now part of Co. Leitrim from the thirteenth century. *Mac Giolla na Naomh* was principally a south Connacht name, while *Ó Fuaráin* originated in Co. Cork. The name is still most common in Cork, though large numbers are also to be found in the Connacht counties of Galway and Mayo, as well as in Dublin.

FOX

Fox is a common English surname, based on a nickname, and a significant number of Irish bearers of the name will be of English descent. In the majority of cases, however, Fox is a simple translation of *Ó* or *Mac an tSionnaigh*, 'descendant' or 'son of the fox' respectively. From early times the *Mac an tSionnaigh* were widely scattered, allowing their name to be anglicised phonetically in an extraordinary number of ways depending on local accents and dialects – MacAshinna, MacShanaghy, Shinny, Shannon, Shinnock, Tinney and MacAtinna are only some of the variation which have been noted.

Ó Sionnaigh has a more particular history. Tadhg Ó Catharnaigh ('Kearney') was Chief of Teffia in Co. Meath in the eleventh century and, for his wily ways, become known as *'An Sionnach'* the fox. As his descendants prospered even further, becoming proprietors of the entire barony of Kilcoursey in Co. Offaly and acquiring the title 'Barons Kilcoursey', they adopted his nickname as their own surname in place of Ó Catharnaigh, and the chief of the family took on 'The Fox' as a title. They lost their property after the rebellion of 1641-2, but the descent from the last duly inaugurated Chief has remained unbroken. John William Fox, The Fox, Chief of his Name, recognised as such by the Chief Herald of Ireland, lives in Australia.

GALLAGHER

(O')Gallagher in Irish is *Ó Gallcobhar*, from *gall*, meaning 'foreign' and *cabhair*, meaning 'help' or 'support'. The original *Gallcobhar* from whom the family claim descent was himself descended from Conall Gulban, son of Niall of the Nine Hostages, the fifth-century monarch who was reputedly responsible for the kidnapping of St Patrick to Ireland, and who was the founder of the *Uí Néill* dynasty. The O'Gallaghers claim to be the most senior branch of the *Cinéal Conaill*, the group of families who all descend from Conall Gulban. Their territory was in *Tír Chonaill* (literally 'Conall's Land'), in what is now Co. Donegal. From the fourteenth to the sixteenth centuries they were hereditary commanders of the cavalry of the forces of the O'Donnell princes of *Tír Chonaill*. Today Gallagher is the single

FOX

GORMAN

GALLAGHER

most numerous surname in Co. Donegal, and is also very common in the adjoining counties of Derry, Fermanagh and Tyrone. Though less common elsewhere in Ireland, it has spread throughout the country over the centuries.

GORMAN

Gorman is a relatively common name in England, where it is derived from the Middle English personal name Gormund, from *gar*, meaning 'spear', and *mund*,

meaning 'protection'. A few Irish Gormans may be of this connection, but in the vast majority of cases in Ireland the surname comes from the original Irish *Mac Gormáin*, from a diminutive of *gorm*, meaning 'blue'. The original homeland was in Co. Laois, in Slievmargy, but they were dispossessed by the Prestons, a Norman family, and removed to counties Clare and Monaghan. The Clare branch became well known in later years for the extent of their wealth and hospitality, and for their patronage of poetry. From Clare they spread also into the adjoining county of Tipperary. When the native Irish

began to resume the old O and Mac prefixes to their names in the nineteenth century, the Clare family mistakenly became 'O'Gorman', probably following the error of the then best known bearer of the surname, Chevalier Thomas O'Gorman (1725-1808), an Irish exile in France. In Tipperary, the name has generally remained 'Gorman', while in Monaghan the original MacGorman still exists, along with the other two versions.

GRAHAM

Graham is a Scottish surname, deriving from the placename Grantham, also known as Graham, in modern Lincolnshire in England. It was taken to Scotland in the twelfth century by William de Graham, a Norman baron who held the manor of Grantham, and from whom virtually all modern bearers of the name are descended. In Ireland it is overwhelmingly concentrated in Ulster, in particular counties Down and Fermanagh, as well as Armagh, Monaghan and Tyrone. The Irish Grahams are mostly descended from a branch of the family which migrated from Midlothian to the Scottish borders in the Middle Ages and became, with the Armstrongs, the most powerful of the outlaw 'riding clans'. When the power of these clans was savagely broken by James I, many migrated to the north of Ireland, settling especially in Co. Fermanagh. Unlike the other clans, from that base the Grahams spread widely through the surrounding counties.

GREENE

Green(e) is an extremely common English surname, generally referring to someone who lived near a village green. Many Irish bearers of the name, particularly in Ulster, are probably of this connection. However, Green(e) was also used as the anglicised version of a wide variety of Irish names containing *uaithne*, 'green', or *glas*, 'grey-green'. *Ó hUaithnigh*, anglicised as both 'Green' and the phonetic 'Hooney', arose in Co. Cork. In Co. Clare the original, from the same Irish stem, was *Ó hUaithnigh*, more rarely anglicised as 'Hooneen' and 'Huneen'. In Ulster, *Mac Glaisín*, 'McGlashan', and *Mac Giolla Ghlais*, 'McAlesher', relatively common in counties Antrim and Derry, also became Green. Further,

A tiny, hand-carved heraldic gemstone showing arms associated with families of the name Greene in Ireland.

Ó Griana, Mac Griana, found in northwest Ulster, and *Ó Grianáin*, from counties Cavan and Sligo, were also phonetically rendered as Green, although the root of the names is the Irish *grian*, meaning 'sun'.

GRIFFIN

While the name is English in appearance, in the great majority of cases Irish Griffins are descended from the *Ó Gríobhtha*. Both the English and Irish versions ultimately have the same source, the name of the legendary monster, the gryphon, used as a nickname for someone fierce or dangerous. The name arose separately in at least two areas: in Co. Kerry, centred on Ballygriffin in Glanarought barony, and in Co. Clare, where the seat was at Ballygriffy, near Ennis. From these two starting points the families spread and intermingled, and today Griffin is among the 100 most common Irish

GRIFFIN

surnames, found principally in the original homelands of Clare and Kerry, as well as in the adjoining counties of Cork and Limerick.

HALL

Hall is an extremely common English surname, found widely in Scotland also, denoting someone who lived near a large house, or who was employed in a manor or hall. In Ireland, it is most common in Ulster, where its source is predominantly Scottish; the Halls were one of the outlaw 'riding clans' who migrated to Ulster when their dominance over the Scottish Borders was broken by James I. The name is particularly associated with Co. Antrim. Elsewhere, it is also found in Munster, brought during the sixteenth and seventeenth century plantations, and in Leinster, due to the long association of parts of that province with English rule. It is rare in the western province of Connacht.

HAMILTON

The surname is one of the most common and famous in Scotland, coming from the Norman baron Walter Fitzgilbert de Hameldone, a supporter of Robert the Bruce in the fourteenth century. His name came from the now deserted village of Hameldone (Old English *hamel*, 'crooked', and *dun*, 'hill') in the parish of Barkby in Leicestershire. The arrival of Hamiltons in Ireland is inextricably linked to the Plantation of Ulster in the seventeenth century, when a large number of the powerful Scottish landowners granted territory in the province were members of that family. They gained possession of vast tracts of land in counties Armagh, Cavan, Fermanagh and Tyrone, and settled many of their kinsmen on these estates. Sir Frederick Hamilton fought in the army of the Swedish King Gustavus Adolphus before settling in Ulster, and his grandson Gustavus Hamilton was created Viscount Boyne in 1717.

The arms of Limerick city, one of the areas where the surname Hayes originated.

HAYES

Hayes is a common surname in England, where it derives from various places of the same name and from the Norman De la Haye, but in Ireland it is almost always the most common anglicisation of the Irish *Ó hAodha*, from the personal name *Aodh*, 'fire', which was very popular in early Ireland. No doubt this popularity accounts for the fact that the surname originated separately in at least twelve different locations, including southwest Cork, Limerick/Tipperary, south Donegal, Sligo, Monaghan, Meath, Mayo, north Tyrone, south Down, Armagh, and Wexford. As well as Hayes, the surname was also anglicised

as 'O'Hea', particularly in southwest Cork, and as 'Hughes', since *Aodh* was invariably translated as 'Hugh'. This last anglicisation is most common among the five septs originating in the Ulster counties.

HEALY

There is an English surname Healy, derived from the Old English *heah*, 'high', and *leah*, 'clearing', 'wood', but almost all of those bearing the name in Ireland are descendants of one of two Irish families, the *Ó hÉilídhe*, from *éilídhe*, 'claimant', and the *Ó hÉaladaighthe*, from *ealadhach*, 'ingenious'. The *Ó hÉilídhe* had territory in southeast Co. Sligo, on the shores of Lough Arrow, one of the most beautiful parts of the country, where their seat was at Ballyhely. The *Ó hÉaladaighthe*, whose name was originally given the more phonetically accurate equivalent 'Healihy', were based in the parish of Donoghmore in Muskerry in Co. Cork, where they retained considerable power and wealth up to the seventeenth century. The surname is very common and widespread today, though significant concentrations are to be found around the original homelands in Connacht and Cork. The best-known modern bearer of the name was the journalist, John Healy, of the Connacht family, renowned for his passionate defence of the rural way of life.

HEGARTY

In Irish the surname is *Ó hÉigceartaigh*, from *éigceartach*, meaning 'unjust'. The name appears to have arisen first in the area now divided between counties Derry and Donegal, where the *Ó hÉigceartaigh* were a branch of the Cinel Eoghain, that large group of families claiming descent from Eoghan, one of the sons of Niall of the Nine Hostages, the fifth-century monarch who supposedly kidnapped St Patrick to Ireland. However, today the surname is much more common in Co. Cork, at the other end of the country. Traditionally, the Cork (O')Hegartys were claimed as a branch of the more historically prominent northern family, but *ecertach* was a common personal name in Munster, and it seems more likely that the surname arose separately there. At

HEGARTY

any rate, O'Hegartys are recorded in west Cork as early as the thirteenth century, and remain strongly associated with the area.

HENNESSY

The original Irish form of the name is *Ó hAonghasa*, from the personal name *Aonghas*, anglicised 'Angus', one of the pre-Christian Celtic gods. This was quite popular, and it gave rise to the surname in several distinct localities: in the north of the present Co. Offaly, from where the family later spread into the adjoining counties of Clare and Tipperary; in southwest Co. Cork, where they formed part of the *Corca Laoidhe* tribal grouping, descended from pre-Gaelic origins, and in east Cork, in the territory between the present towns of

HENNESSY   HICKEY

Fermoy and Mitchelstown. The east Cork family produced the most famous bearer of the name, Richard Hennessy (1720-1800), who fought with Dillon's Brigade in the French army, and founded the famous brandy distillery in 1765. Today the surname is still strongly associated with Co. Cork, though significant numbers also appear in counties Limerick, Tipperary and Clare. In the latter area, the name has also been anglicised as 'Henchy' and 'Hensey'.

HENRY

There are several Irish, Scottish and Norman originals for this surname. In Munster it is often the anglicisation of *Mac Innéirghe*, from *innéireighe*, meaning 'abandonment', and has also been rendered into English as MacHenry and MacEnery. This family were prominent in Co. Limerick. In Co. Tyrone, it is found as an anglicisation of *Ó hInneirghe*, from the same root. At least two other Gaelic Irish sources for the name exist in Ulster, the *Mac Éinrí*, descended from Henry, son of

Dermot O'Cahan (died 1428), situated in the north Antrim/Derry area, and the *Ó hAiniarriadh*, originally from southeast Ulster. In addition, the surname appears in Connacht, where it seems to derive from a branch of the Norman FitzHenrys, who settled in west Galway in the Middle Ages. To complicate matters further, Ulster contains many Scottish surnames based on Henry as a personal name – Henderson, Hendry, McKendry, Hendron etc. – which have long been confused with similar-sounding Gaelic Irish surnames in the same areas.

HICKEY

The original Irish for Hickey is *Ó hIcidhe*, from *iceadh*, meaning 'healer'. The Hickeys were part of the tribal grouping, the *Dál gCais*, which produced Brian Boru, the High King of Ireland who defeated the Vikings in 1014. This grouping had its territory in the area now part of Co. Clare and north Tipperary, and it is this area with which the Hickeys remain closely identified. Their

HIGGINS

HOGAN

surname arose because of their position as hereditary physicians to the royal O'Brien family. From their original homeland, the name spread first into the neighbouring Co. Limerick, and from there even wider, so that Hickey is today one of the most common and widespread of Irish surnames.

HIGGINS

In form, Higgins is an English name, from the medieval given name 'Higgin', a diminutive of 'Hicke', which was in turn a pet form of Richard. In Ireland, however, the vast majority of those bearing the name are of Gaelic Irish stock, Higgins being used as an anglicisation of the Irish *Ó hUigín*, from *uiginn*, meaning 'Viking'. The original *Uigin* from whom they claim descent was grandson to Niall of the Nine Hostages, the fifth-century king who

founded the powerful tribal grouping the *Uí Néill*, and they are therefore regarded as part of that grouping. Originally based in the midlands, part of the southern *Uí Néill*, they moved west over the centuries to Sligo and Mayo, and more than half of those bearing the surname today still live in the western province of Connacht. Don Ambrosio O'Higgins rose to become Viceroy of Peru for Spain, and his son, Bernardo, is widely remembered in South America as the 'Liberator of Chile'. Ambrosio was born in Ballinvary, Co. Sligo, and took the Spanish title Baron de Valenar, Baron Ballinvary.

HOGAN

The Irish version of the surname is *Ó hÓgáin*, from a diminutive of *óg*, meaning 'young'. The original *Ógán* from whom the family claim descent lived in the tenth century and was an uncle of Brian Boru, the High King who defeated the Vikings at Clontarf in 1014. Like Brian Boru, they were part of the *Dál gCais* tribal grouping, whose original territory took in Clare and parts of Tipperary. The (O')Hogans were centred on Ardcrony, near the modern town of Nenagh in north Tipperary, where their chief had his seat. From there the surname spread far and wide, and is today one of the most common in Ireland, with particular concentrations close to the first homeland, in counties Clare, Tipperary and Limerick. In addition, significant numbers are to be found in Cork, where it is thought that the name may have had a separate origin, in the southwest of that county.

HUGHES

Hughes is common in England and Wales, where it is a patronymic, deriving from the father's name, and quite a few Irish bearing the name, particularly in Ulster, will be of English and Welsh stock. Elsewhere, it is almost always one of the anglicisations of the Irish *Ó hAodha*, from the personal name *Aodh*, 'fire', the second most popular such anglicisation after 'Hayes', since *Aodh* was invariably translated as 'Hugh'. Perhaps because of the example of the settlers, Hughes was the most frequent anglicisation amongst the Gaelic Irish in Ulster, where there were *Ó hAodha* at Ballyshannon (Co. Donegal), Ardstraw (Co. Tyrone), Tynan (Co. Armagh), Farney (Co. Monaghan), and south Co. Down. In places, too, Hughes became the English version of *Mac Aoidh* or *Mac Aodha*, more usually given as Magee or McHugh.

HURLEY

Hurley has become the English version of at least three distinct original Irish names: the *Ó hUirthile*, part of the *Dál gCais* tribal group, based in Clare and north Tipperary; the *Ó Muirthile*, based around Kilbritain in west Cork; and the *Ó hIarlatha*, from the district of Ballyvourney, also in Cork, whose name is more usually anglicised '(O')Herlihy'. The principal concentrations of Hurleys are today found in counties Tipperary and Limerick, where they spread from the original Dalcassian homeland, and in Cork. An interesting example of the pseudo-translation of surnames is found in Clare, where

HURLEY

some whose name was originally Hurley have now become 'Commane', since the Irish for the hurley-stick used in the sport of hurling is *camán*.

JOHNSTON

In form at least the surname is Scottish, deriving from the place of the same name in Annandale in Dumfriesshire, which was originally 'John's town'. The original John was a Norman landowner in the area in the twelfth century, and instead of taking on the straightforward patronymic 'Johnson', his descendants adopted the placename as their surname, becoming Johnston(e)s. This family, the source of virtually all Scottish bearers of the name, became one of the strongest and most unruly of the Border clans, and their long feud with another clan, the Maxwells, was notorious for its ferocity. When the clans were eventually 'pacified' and scattered by James II, many Johnstons fled to Ulster where, like large numbers from the other clans – Elliots, Armstrongs, Nixons and others – they settled mainly in Co. Fermanagh, where the surname is today the second most numerous in the county. As well as these Johnstons, however, many others whose name was originally Johnson adopted the Scottish name. Such adoptions occurred predominantly in Ulster, and affected those of Scottish and of native Irish origin, with the MacIans of Caithness translating their surname as Johnson, and then altering it to Johnston in many cases, and the MacShanes of the Armagh/Tyrone district, a branch of the O'Neills, doing likewise.

JONES

Jones is an extremely common surname in England and Wales, one of the wide range of names derived from the personal name 'John'. It is a patronymic, coming from the genitive form 'John's'. Its widespread popularity in Wales is due to the form adopted in the Welsh translation of the Authorized Version of the Bible, *Ioan*, phonetically close to the modern surname. In Ireland it is quite widespread, coming among the two hundred most frequent names, and is understandably most closely associated with areas where English influence was strongest.

JOYCE

Joyce derives from the Breton personal name *Iodoc*, a diminutive of *iudh*, meaning 'lord', which was adopted by the Normans as *Josse*. A number of English surnames arose from this Norman original, including Joce, Joass, and Joyce, this last being far more frequent in Ireland than anywhere else. The first bearer of the name in Ireland was a Thomas de Joise, of Norman Welsh extraction, who married a daughter of the O'Brien Princes of Thomond in 1283, and settled in the far west of Connacht, on the borders of the modern counties of Mayo and Galway. Their descendants became completely gaelicised, ruling that territory, today still known as 'Joyce's Country', down to the seventeenth century. The surname remains strongly associated with

JOYCE

the area, with a large majority of Joyces originating in counties Galway and Mayo. The most famous modern bearer of the name was James Joyce (1882-1941), author of *Dubliners*, *Portrait of the Artist as a Young Man*, *Ulysses*, and *Finnegans Wake*, said to have been the only twentieth-century novelist to publish nothing but masterpieces.

KANE

Kane and O'Kane are the most common anglicised versions of the Irish *Ó Catháin*, from a diminutive of *cath*, meaning 'battle'. Kane and O'Kane are most frequent in Ulster, where *Ó Catháin* arose as a surname in the Laggan district of east Donegal, as part of the *Cinéal Eoghain*, the large group of families descended from Eoghan, son of Niall of the Nine Hostages, the fifth-century monarch who founded the *Uí Néill* dynasty and was supposedly responsible for the kidnapping of St Patrick to Ireland. In the twelfth century these Ulster *Ó Catháin* conquered a large territory to the east of their original homeland around Coleraine and Keenaght in what is now Co. Derry, and remained powerful and

The Giant's Causeway, near Portrush in Co. Antrim, is one of the natural wonders of Ireland. From the thirteenth century the *Ó Catháin* were among the most powerful and numerous of the families in the area.

important in that area down to the wars of the seventeenth century. Their last chief died in the Tower of London in 1628. Two other common surnames, McClosky and McAvinney, are offshoots of *Ó Catháin*, stemming respectively from the twelfth-century *Bloskey Ó Catháin*, and *Aibhne Ó Catháin*. Kane remains particularly common in the Coleraine district of Co. Derry, and in the adjoining county of Antrim.

KAVANAGH

Kavanagh, along with its variants Cavanagh, Cavanaugh etc., is the English version of *Caomhánach*, one of the very few Gaelic Irish surnames not to include 'O' or 'Mac'. It means 'follower of (St) Caomhán', a name which is itself a diminutive of *caomh*, meaning 'gentle' or 'tender'. It was first borne as a surname in the twelfth century by Dónal, illegitimate son of Dermot MacMurrough, King of Leinster. He became known as 'Dónal Caomhánach' through having been fostered by a successor of the saint based probably at Kilcavan in Bannow parish in south Co. Wexford.

Patrick Kavanagh (1904-1967), who was the first poet of modern Ireland to give voice to the realities of life in the new state, as well as being a powerful polemicist.

KEANE

Like Kane, Keane is an anglicisation of *Ó Catháin*, from a diminutive of *cath*, meaning 'battle'. As an anglicisation, however, it is much more common in Connacht than in Ulster, the homeland of the Kanes. This is because *Ó Catháin* arose separately as a surname in Co. Galway, where the family were a branch of the historic *Uí*

KAVANAGH

KEANE

Although this Dónal was the first bearer of the name, in fact the majority of the Kavanagh septs that proliferated from the fifteenth century on descend from Art MacMurrough Kavanagh, King of Leinster, who died in 1418. The territory of the Kavanaghs at this period was huge, comprising nearly all of the modern Co. Carlow, and most of north and northwest Co. Wexford. This was known as 'the Kavanaghs' country' and with good reason: Art held complete control over it, even receiving dues from the English crown, the 'black rent' as it was known. The chiefs of the family continued to take the ruling title MacMurrough, but by the mid-sixteenth century their power was on the wane, and was decisively broken by the start of the seventeenth century, when English rule was established and north Wexford planted with English settlers.

Despite their loss of power and property, the line of descent from the last duly inaugurated Chief of the Name, Brian Kavanagh, the MacMorrough, remains unbroken; the title is now held by his descendant Andrew MacMorrogh Kavanagh of Borris, Co. Carlow.

The most famous modern bearer of the name was

Fiachra tribal grouping. Traditionally it has been believed that the prominent Clare Keanes were an offshoot of the Ulster *Ó Catháin*, but the closeness of Clare and Galway must make this doubtful. A distinct family, the *Ó Céin* from Co. Waterford have anglicised their name as 'Kean', but without the final 'e'. The famous actors Edmund Kean (1787-1833) and his son Charles (1811-1880) were of this family.

KEARNEY

KEARNEY

Kearney is common and widespread in Ireland, and has a number of different origins. In the west it originated in Co. Mayo, near Moynulla and Balla, the territory of the *Ó Cearnaigh* (from *cearnach*, meaning 'victorious'), where it has sometimes also been anglicised as Carney. A separate family of the same name, but anglicised as (O)Kearney, arose in Clare, and migrated in early times to the area around Cashel in Co. Tipperary. In Ulster the name derives from *Mac Cearnaigh*, also from *cearnach*; they were part of the *Cinéal Eoghain*, the large group of

families descended from Eoghan, son of Niall of the Nine Hostages, the fifth-century monarch who founded the *Uí Néill* dynasty and was supposedly responsible for the kidnapping of St Patrick to Ireland. The most historically important family, however, were the *Ó Catharnaigh*, from *catharnach*, meaning 'warlike'. These were chiefs of a large territory in the midlands, in the modern counties of Meath and Offaly; one of their number became Baron Kilcoursey, from the placename in Offaly. The composer of the Irish national anthem was Peadar Kearney (1883-1942).

KEATING

Although Keating is found as a surname in England, where it derives from the Old English *Cyting*, from *cyt*, meaning 'kite', in Ireland it is almost always of Norman origin. The family arrived with the Cambro-Norman invaders in the twelfth century and soon became thoroughly Irish, settling in south Leinster, and particularly in Co. Wexford, where the name is still very common. The most famous historical bearer of the name was Geoffrey Keating (or *Seathrún Céitinn*) the poet and historian who lived in the first half of the seventeenth century and wrote *Foras Feasa ar Éirinn,* a narrative history of the country defending it against the accounts given by foreign writers. In modern times the painter Seán Keating (1889-1977) specialised in traditional scenes, and was president of the Royal Hibernian Academy for fourteen years.

KELLEHER

Kelleher, and its variants Keliher, Kellaher etc., are the English versions of the Irish name *Ó Céileachair*, from *céileachar*, meaning 'uxorious', 'overly fond of one's wife'. The original *Céileachar* from whom the family claim descent was a nephew of Brian Boru, and part of the famous *Dál gCais* tribal grouping. Although the family originated in Clare, homeland of the *Dál gCais*, they migrated southeast to Co. Cork in the fourteenth century and it is now in that county and the adjoining Co. Kerry that the surname is most frequently found. It is sometimes abbreviated to 'Keller', a name more usually associated with Germany, and in this form is recorded in Co. Cork.

KELLY

Kelly comes from the Irish *Ó Ceallaigh*, based on the popular personal name Ceallach, which may mean either 'bright-haired' or 'troublesome'. The popularity of the name meant that it was incorporated into permanent surnames in between seven and ten different places, including Co. Meath, north Wicklow, the Antrim/Derry area, Co. Sligo, Galway/Roscommon, north Down and Co. Laois

KEATING

KELLY

The most prominent of these families are the O'Kellys of *Uí Máine*, or Hy Many, an ancient territory taking in east Galway and south Roscommon, also known simply as 'O'Kelly's Country'. Their pedigree takes them back to Máine Mór, first chief of the area bearing his name, who lived in the fifth century. His descendant Ceallach (died *c.*874) was the twelfth chief, and it is from him that the surname derives. His great-great-grandson Tadhg Mór, who died at the battle of Clontarf in 1014, was the first to use the name in true hereditary fashion.

Despite the loss of most of their possessions in the catastrophic wars of the seventeenth century, a loss shared with most of the rest of the Gaelic aristocracy, the succession to the position of head of the sept has continued unbroken down to the present incumbent, Walter Lionel O'Kelly of Gallagh and Tycooly, Count of the Holy Roman Empire, known as 'the O'Kelly', and recognised as such by the Chief Herald of Ireland.

Today, Kelly and O'Kelly are almost as numerous in Ireland as Murphy, and are to be found throughout Ireland. Individuals of the name have been prominent in all spheres of Irish life. The best-known modern Irish sculptor was Oisín Kelly (1915-1981); Charles E. Kelly (1902-1981) was one of the founders of *Dublin Opinion*, the most famous satirical magazine to appear in Ireland, and James O'Kelly (1845-1916) had a remarkable career as a war correspondent and member of Parliament.

KENNEDY

Kennedy in Irish is *Ó Cinnéide*, from a compound word meaning 'ugly-headed' or 'rough-headed'. The original bearer of the name, from whom the family claim descent,

A brass seal in the shape of a monk, with the O'Kelly arms.

KENNEDY

KEOGH

was a nephew of Brian Boru. His descendants were one of the most powerful families in the famous *Dál gCais* tribal grouping, and migrated from their homeland near Killaloe in Clare into adjoining north Tipperary, to become Lords of Ormond for over four hundred years up to the sixteenth century. From there the surname spread farther afield, becoming one of the most numerous and widespread in Ireland. In Ulster, many Kennedys are originally of Scottish stock, the MacKennedys being a branch of the Clan Cameron. The surname is now also very common in Galloway and Ayrshire. The most famous modern bearer of the name was, of course, John F. Kennedy, thirty-fifth president of the U.S., descended from a Wexford branch of the Dalcassian family.

KENNY

In Irish Kenny is generally *Ó Cionaodha*, from the personal name *Cionaodh*, of uncertain origin. It was borne by a high-king of Ireland *Cionaodh mac Irgalaig* in the eight century, and seems to have become popular after this. At any rate *Ó Cionaodha* arose as a separate surname in a number of places, including Co. Tyrone,

and the Galway/Roscommon region. This latter family was the most important historically, lords of Munter Kenny, and it is from them that the majority of Irish Kennys spring. In Ulster, Kenny was also the anglicisation of the separate *Ó Coinne*, based in Co. Down, and became a synonym for a number of other names, including McKenna, Canning and Keaney. The stage designer and director Sean Kenny (1933-1973) had achieved international fame when he died suddenly.

KEOGH

Keogh, and its variant Kehoe, are the anglicisations of the Irish *Mac Eochaidh*, from *eoch*, meaning 'horse'. It arose as a surname in three distinct areas. The first was in south Roscommon, around Moyfinn in the barony of Athlone, which used to be known as 'Keogh's country'. This family was part of the *Uí Máine* tribal grouping. The second was in west Tipperary, near Limerick city; the placename Ballymackeogh marks the centre of their territory. The third and most important, both numerically and historically, was in Leinster, where the original homeland was in north Kildare, whence they migrated first to Wicklow and then south to Wexford. It is in

Above: the Kennedy family in 1934, with (front) Patricia, Mr and Mrs Joseph Kennedy with baby Edward, Kathleen, Eunice and Rosemary, and (rear) John F., Jeanne and Robert. Right: tartan of the Scottish Kerrs.

Wexford that the name has been most commonly anglicised Kehoe. The surname is now most frequent in Leinster, though it has become widespread throughout Ireland.

KERR

Kerr is Scottish and northern English in origin, describing a person who lived near overgrown marshland, *kerr* in northern Middle English. As might be expected, it is principally found in Ulster, where the majority of those bearing the name are descended from one of the Scottish

Border riding clans, whose enforced migration in the seventeenth century also brought large numbers of Armstrongs, Johnstones and others to the province, where they settled, initially at least in Co. Fermanagh. A separate Scottish family of the name is part of the Clan Campbell in Argyllshire. As well as these Scottish origins, however, Kerr (along with Carr) was used as the anglicisation of a number of native Ulster names, including *Mac Giolla Chathair* and *Mac Ciaráin* (Kerin) in Donegal, *Ó Cairre* and *Mac Cairre* in Co. Armagh, and *Mac Giolla Cheara* in Co. Monaghan.

The arms of Galway, where the surname *Mac Conraoi* became 'King', and where the name is now most common.

many, though not all of those of the name, will be of English stock, bearing the English surname which originated simply as a description of someone of kingly bearing. The majority, however, are of native Irish origin, since King was used as a (mis)translation of a number of Irish names which contained sounds similar to *rí*, 'king'. Among the many such names are *Mac Fhearadhaigh* ('McAree/McGarry') in Co. Monaghan, *Ó Maolconaire* and *Ó Conraoi* ('Conroy/Conry') in Co. Roscommon, *Mac Conraoi*, ('Conroy') in Co. Galway (where the change to King was almost total), *Ó Conaire* ('Connery') in Munster. In Ulster, in counties Antrim, Tyrone and Down, *Mac Fhinn* ('Maginn') was also changed, by phonetic misrepresentation rather than mistranslation, to King.

The arms of Ennis, in the heart of the territory where the surname Kiely originated.

KIELY

Kiely is the anglicised version of the Irish *Ó Cadhla*, from *cadhla*, meaning 'beautiful'. It was popular as a personal name among the tribal grouping the *Dál gCais*, who acquired the high-kingship of Ireland under Brian Boru in the eleventh century. Their base was in the Clare/Limerick area, and this is the part of the country in which the surname is still most numerous, although it has now spread widely throughout Munster. The best known contemporary bearer of the surname in Ireland is the journalist and novelist Benedict Kiely, whose stories and essays are well-loved for their relaxed, anecdotal style.

LEARY

Leary and O'Leary derive from the original Irish *Ó Laoghaire*, from *Laoghaire*, meaning 'a keeper of calves'. Although there was a fifth-century king who gave his name to *Dún Laoghaire*, the port south of Dublin, no connection exists with the surname, which originated in Co. Cork and is even today to be found predominantly in that area. The family originally inhabited the rocky sea-coast of southwest cork, between Roscarbery and Glandore, but the coming of the Normans displaced them, and they migrated to the mountains of Iveleary, which now incorporates their name, where they were and are particularly associated with the district of Inchigeelagh.

KING

King is one of the most common surnames in Ireland, and is distributed throughout the country. In Ulster,

LEE

In appearance Lee is a common English name, used either for a person who lived near a pasture or meadow, from the Old English *lea*, or for a person from one of the many places so called, such as Lea in Shropshire, and many bearing the name in Ireland today will be descended from English settlers. In the majority of cases, however, Lee is the anglicised version of a number of original Irish names: *Ó Laoidhigh*, from *laoidheach*, meaning 'poet' or 'poetic', which arose separately in Connacht in west Galway, and in the south in the Cork/Limerick area, and *Mac Laoidhigh*, ('McLee') from the same stem, which is found in Co. Laois. In Ulster *Mac an Leágha* ('McAlee'), was also sometimes anglicised as Lee, as was, in Co. Monaghan, *Mac Giolla Eachaidh* ('McCloy'). The most historically notable of the families were the O'Lees of Galway, powerful subchieftains under the O'Flahertys.

LEARY

LENEHAN

Lenehan is the anglicised version of the Irish *Ó Leannacháin*, possibly from *leannach*, meaning 'sorrowful'. It appears to have arisen separately in two localities, in Co. Roscommon in the west, and in the south in the Limerick/Tipperary region. Bearers of the surname are found in both areas today, but it is most common in the south. The most prominent contemporaries of the name are Brian Lenihan (b.1924) and his younger sister Mrs Mary O'Rourke, of the Roscommon family, who both served in a variety of ministerial positions in the Irish government from the 1970s to the 1990s.

LENNON

Lennon is primarily the anglicised form of the Irish *Ó Leannáin*, from *leannán*, meaning 'lover'. However, *Ó Leannáin* has also sometimes been anglicised as 'Linnane' or even 'Leonard'. Additional uncertainty is caused by the fact that Lennon has occasionally been used as the English version of completely different Irish surnames, in particular *Ó Lonáin* or *Ó Lonagáin* ('Lenane' or 'Lannigan') based in west Cork, and *Ó Luinigh* ('Lunney') originally from Donegal and now strongly associated with the adjoining Co. Fermanagh. The primary Irish source of Lennon, *Ó Leannáin*, arose separately in east Co. Galway, in Co. Mayo, and in Co. Fermanagh. Historically, the most important were the Fermanagh family, who held land and ecclesiastical office in the parish of Inishmacsaint. Today, Lennon remains common in Ulster, but elsewhere has spread from its traditional homelands to become most frequent in the eastern province of Leinster.

LONG

In appearance at least Long is a typical English or Scottish name, derived from a nickname for a tall person. In addition, the Norman names *de Lung* and *de Long* have become 'Long' over the centuries. No doubt many in Ireland bearing the surname today are of English, Scottish or Norman descent. However, there were also two native Gaelic families, the *Ó Longáin* and the *Ó Longaigh*, whose name have been anglicised Long.

LYNCH

Ó Longáin, also anglicised as 'Langan', arose initially in Co. Armagh, but quickly spread throughout the northern counties, and is now most common in Ulster in Co. Donegal. It seems likely that it shares its probable linguistic origin with *Ó Longaigh*, deriving from *long*, 'ship', and therefore meaning 'seafarer'.

Ó Longaigh arose in the south of the country, in Co. Cork. The earliest records of the family, dating from the fourteenth century, show them as prosperous hereditary occupiers of church lands in the parish of Cannovee, in the barony of Muskerry in mid-Cork. This, together with the neighbouring parish of Moviddy, is the area with which the family remain most strongly associated down to the present. They took part on the losing side in the wars of the seventeenth century and, like virtually all of the native aristocracy, lost their possessions. Unlike most of the others, however, the descent from the last duly inaugurated Chief of the Name, Dermod O'Longy, remains unbroken. The official title is 'O'Long of Garrenelongy', referring to a townland in the parish of Moviddy, and the current holder, officially recognised by the Chief Herald of Ireland, is Denis Long.

LYNCH

Lynch, which is today one of the most common surnames throughout Ireland, is unusual in that it has two completely distinct origins. The first is Norman, from *de Lench,* possibly derived from a placename now forgotten. The family settled initially in Co. Meath, and a branch then established itself in Galway, where they rapidly became one of the strongest of the 'Tribes of Galway'; one of their number, James Lynch, mayor in 1493, is reputed to have hanged his own son for murder when no one else could be found to carry out the sentence. The arms illustrated are for this family. The second origin for the name is Gaelic, from the Irish *Ó Loingsigh*, from *loingseach*, meaning 'seaman'. This arose quite separately in a number of areas, including Clare/Limerick, Sligo, west Cork, Cavan, Donegal and the north Antrim/Derry region, where they were chiefs of the old kingdom of *Dál Riada* in medieval times. As the variety of geographical sources implies, the Gaelic origin is responsible for the wide frequency of the surname today.

The arms of Castlebar, Co. Mayo, close to the western region where the surname Lyons originated.

LYONS

Lyons is one of the commonest surnames in Ireland, particularly in the three southern provinces. In Ulster especially it may be a variant of the English and Scottish surname 'Lyon', which can derive, as a nickname, from 'lion', from the first name Leo or Leon, or from the place-name Lyon-la-Forêt in Normandy. Elsewhere, however,

Lyons is virtually always the anglicised version of one of two Irish names, *Ó Laighin*, from *laighean*, meaning 'spear', or *Ó Liatháin*, possibly from *liath*, meaning 'grey'. *Ó Laighin* originated in two areas, in Co. Kerry and in east Co. Galway, where the family's territory was centred on Kilconnell. In Kerry, however, the name was almost invariably anglicised as 'Lyne'. The *Ó Liatháin* family are reputed to have originated in Co. Limerick, but are now to be found much more frequently in Co. Cork, particularly in the north of the county, where the village of Castlelyons records their presence. *Ó Liatháin* has also been anglicised as 'Lehane'.

MACAULEY

MACAULEY

MacAuley and its many variants – Cawley, Gawley, Macauley, Magawley etc. – may be either Scottish or Irish in origin. They are anglicisations of two distinct Irish surnames, *Mac Amhalgaidh* ('son of Auley') and *Mac Amhlaoibh* ('son of Auliff'). The former derives from a native personal name now obsolete, and the

family bearing the surname were rulers of a territory in what is now Offaly/Westmeath. The latter derives from a Gaelic version of the common Norse name 'Olaf', and the family claim descent from *Amhlaoibh,* son of the first Maguire king of Fermanagh, who ruled at the end of the thirteenth century. They gave their name to the barony of Clanawley in that county. An entirely distinct family, the MacAuliffs of Munster, are descended from Amhlaoibh MacCarthy. In Scotland also the surname and its variants have the same two distinct origins, from the Gaelic and Norse personal names. The Scottish origin is most common in the northeast of Ulster, where a branch of the Dumbartonshire MacAuleys settled in the sixteenth century.

MACBRIDE

MacBride comes from the Irish *Mac Giolla Bhríghde*, 'son of the follower of (St) Bridget'; St Bridget was a famous abbess of Kildare, who died in 525. Also derived from the same Irish original are the surnames Kilbride, Gilbride, MacIlvreed, MacGilbride and others. The principal Irish family of the name were based in the north of Co. Donegal in Raymunterdoney, where they were very prominent in the church, a number of the family becoming bishops. A branch migrated to Co. Down in early times, where the surname remains quite numerous. In Ulster also, the name may have a Scottish origin, from the descendants of one Gillebride, progenitor of one branch of the Clan Donald. The best known contemporary bearer of the surname was Sean MacBride (1904-1988), active on the Republican side in the War of Independence and after, Minister for External Affairs from 1948 to 1951, founder-member of Amnesty International, winner of the Nobel Peace Prize in 1974, the Lenin Peace Prize in 1977 and the American Medal for Justice in 1978.

MACCABE

MacCabe derives from the Irish *Mac Cába*, from *cába* meaning 'cape' or 'cloak'. The family are thought originally to have been a branch of the MacLeods of Harris in the Hebrides. They came to Ireland from there in the mid-fourteenth century to act as gallowglasses (mercenaries) to the O'Reillys and the O'Rourkes, the

MACCABE

MCCANN

ruling families in the kingdom of Breffny, the territory now part of counties Longford and Cavan. They became completely hibernicized and adopted the customs and practices of the Irish, including internecine war; having established themselves in neighbouring Fermanagh by the fifteenth century, they continued the struggle for control with the Maguires up to the final catastrophe of the seventeenth century. The surname also became prominent in other adjoining counties, in particular Co. Monaghan.

MCCANN

There is dispute as to whether McCann comes from the Irish *Mac Anna*, 'son of Annadh', or *Mac Cana*, from *cana*, meaning 'wolf cub'. At any rate, the major family of the name were known as lords of Clanbrassil, an area on the southern shores of Lough Neagh in the modern Co. Armagh, which they conquered from the O'Garveys. They appear to have been a branch of the *Cinéal Eoghain*, the large group of families claiming descent from Eoghan, one of the sons of Niall of the Nine Hostages, the fifth century founder of the *Uí Néill* dynasty. The death in 1155 of one of their chiefs, Amhlaoibh Mac

Cana, is recorded in the Annals of the Four Masters with praise for his chivalry, his vigour, and the fine strong drink he made from the apples in his orchard. Today, the surname is found principally in counties Armagh, Tyrone and Antrim, though it has also spread southwards into the provinces of Leinster and Connacht.

MACCARTHY

MacCarthy comes from the Irish *Mac Cárthaigh*, from *cárthach*, meaning 'loving'. The original Carthach from whom the surname is taken was king of Cashel *c*.1040, at a time when Donncha, son of Brian Boru, was king of Munster. Carthach was part of the dynasty claiming descent from Eoghan, one of the sons of Oiloll Ollum, the semi-legendary, third-century king of Munster. The *Eoghanacht*, as they were known, had dominated Munster virtually unchallenged until the meteoric rise of Brian, part of the rival *Dál gCais*, who claimed descent from Cas, another son of Oiloll Ollum. The *Eoghanacht* resisted the *Dál gCais* fiercely, with the result that the MacCarthys and the O'Briens, with their respective allies, waged bitter, intermittent war on each other for almost a century and a half. In the middle of the twelfth century, the struggle was finally resolved with the expulsion of the MacCarthys from their homeland in the Golden Vale in Co. Tipperary. They moved south, into the historic territory of Desmond, and it is with this area, which includes the modern counties of Cork and Kerry, that they have been most strongly associated ever since.

Despite their displacement, the MacCarthys retained their ability to rule. For almost five centuries they dominated much of Munster, with four distinct branches: those led by the MacCarthy Mór ('Great MacCarthy'), nominal head of all the MacCarthys, who ruled over

MACCARTHY

much of south Kerry; the Duhallow MacCarthys, who controlled northwest Cork; MacCarthy Riabhach ('grey') based in Carbery in southwest Cork; and MacCarthy Muskerry, on the Cork/Kerry border. Each of these families continued resistance to Norman and English encroachment up to the seventeenth century when, like virtually all the Gaelic aristocracy, they lost almost everything. Unlike many others, however, the line of descent of the senior branch was not lost. The current holder of the title MacCarthy Mór, recognised as such by the Chief Herald of Ireland, is Terence MacCarthy, now resident in Morocco.

MACCORMACK

MacCormack and MacCormick are both derived from *Mac Cormaic*, from the extremely popular Irish and Scottish personal name Cormac. This popularity meant that the surname arose independently in a large number of places throughout Ireland (and Scotland), and is today widely scattered. It seems likely also that the

Blarney Castle remained in the possession of the MacCarthys until the end of the seventeenth century, when it passed to the Anglo-Irish Jefferyes family.

creation of these surnames took place at a later date than many of the other native Irish names. The only family of any early consequence were based in Co. Fermanagh, around Kilmacormick, 'MacCormack's church', and were a branch of the Maguires. The most famous bearer of the surname is undoubtedly John MacCormack (1885-1945), the operatic and concert tenor, who achieved extraordinary international fame in the first half of this century.

MACCULLAGH

MacCullagh and MacCullough are very numerous in Ulster, and almost entirely confined to that province. They may have a native Irish, or a Scottish origin. The Irish original is *Mac Con Uladh* or *Mac Cú Uladh*, both meaning 'son of the hound of Ulster', and generally anglicised as MacCullagh, though they also sometimes appear as Coloo, MacAnaul and MacNully. The family were based in east Co. Antrim and north Down. The Scottish origins are various, coming from *Mac Cullaich*, from *cullach*, meaning 'boar', common in Galloway, and from *Mac Lulich*, (*lúlaogh* meaning 'little calf'), which originated in Argyllshire. A member of this latter family was briefly King of Scots. In Scotland, the surname is generally given today as MacCulloch. In Ulster MacCullagh is more common in the west of the province, in particular in Co. Tyrone, while MacCullough appears more frequently in the east, in counties Antrim and Down.

MACDERMOT

MacDermot comes from the Irish *Mac Diarmada*, from the personal name Diarmuid, the meaning of which is uncertain, but may derive from *dia*, 'god' and *armaid* 'of arms'. The individual from whom the surname is taken lived in the twelfth century, and was himself a direct descendant of Maolruanaidh Mór, brother of Conor, King of Connacht, the ancestor of the O'Connors, who ruled in the tenth century. Tradition has it that the two brothers came to an agreement that, in return for surrendering any claim to the kingship of Connacht, Maolruanaidh and his descendants would receive the territory of Moylurg, an area in the north of the modern Co. Roscommon roughly corresponding to the baronies

MACDERMOT

of Boyle and Frenchpark. Certainly this is the area with which the descendants of Maolruanaidh, the MacDermots, have been closely associated down to modern times. For many centuries their seat was a large castle on MacDermot's Island, in Lough Key near the modern town of Boyle

The Moylurg branch remained powerful and influential in their homeland down to the final post-Cromwellian confiscations, when, in common with virtually all of the old Gaelic aristocracy, they were dispossessed of their ancestral lands. Unlike most of the others, however, the MacDermots of Moylurg did manage to salvage some of their old possessions. In the seventeenth century they moved to Coolavin, beside Lough Gara in the neighbouring Co. Sligo, where the line of descent from the original MacDermot chiefs remains unbroken. The current head of the family, known as 'the MacDermot, Prince of Coolavin', and recognised as Chief of his Name by the Chief Herald of Ireland, is Niall Mac Dermot.

Inevitably, as well as the main branch, the MacDermots of Moylurg, a number of other branches also formed over the centuries. The earliest and most prominent of these were the MacDermot Roe ('red') based around Kilronan in Co. Galway, and the

MacDermot Gall ('foreign'), who usurped the chieftainship for a time from their base in east Roscommon. In addition, of course, many other families of the name established themselves over the centuries. The surname is now one of the most common in Ireland, still most frequent in Roscommon, but to be found throughout the island.

MACDONAGH

MacDonagh, and its many variants, MacDonough, Donogh, Donaghy etc., all derive from the Irish *Mac Donnchadha*, from *donnchadh* (often anglicised 'Donagh'), a popular first name meaning 'brown one'. The early popularity of the name meant that the surname

MACDONAGH

based on it arose separately in two places: in Co. Cork, where the MacDonaghs were known as 'Lords of Duhallow', and in Co. Sligo, where the family were rulers in the barony of Tirreril. The Sligo MacDonaghs were in fact a branch of the MacDermotts, claiming Donagh MacDermott as their ancestor. Today the name is rare in Cork, but has become very widespread in the western province of Connacht. The best-known modern bearer of the name is Donagh MacDonagh (1912-1968), the poet, dramatist and lawyer, whose most successful play, *Happy as Larry*, has been translated into a dozen languages.

The MacDonald Tartan

MACDONALD

MacDonald is extremely numerous and widespread throughout Ireland. It is commonly a confusion for MacDonnell (*q.v.*), and shares the same origin, coming from the Gaelic personal name Domhnall, meaning 'world mighty'. However, true MacDonalds are descendants of the Scottish clan of the name. They are

one of the group of Scottish clans who claim descent from Conn of the Hundred Battles, the legendary Irish king, through Colla Uais, who colonised the Hebrides. Their name comes from Donald of Islay, one of the sons of Somhairle, Lord of Argyle. By the fifteenth century they were the most powerful clan in Scotland, controlling the entire western coast of the country. Their involvement in Ireland was continuous from the thirteenth century, when they first arrived as gallowglasses, or mercenaries; such was their fame that they were employed in virtually every local war, spreading and settling throughout the country over the following centuries. Inevitably, their main connection remained with Ulster. A secondary influx into that province of settlers bearing the name occurred in the eighteenth century, when the Highland clearances caused great forced migration from Scotland.

MACDONNELL

MacDonnell, often confused with MacDonald, comes from the Irish *Mac Domhnaill*, from the personal name *Domhnall*, a compound made up of 'world' and 'strong'. It is common and widely distributed throughout Ireland. The principal source of the name outside Ulster is in the old kingdom of Thomond, in the Clare/Limerick area, where the MacDonnells were hereditary poets to the O'Briens. Many other southern MacDonnells will in fact be descendants of MacDonald gallowglasses (*see* MacDonald). In Ulster, the most prominent native family were the MacDonnells of Clankelly, rulers of Fermanagh before the rise of the Maguires. Displaced by their loss of power, they settled in the north of the adjoining Co. Monaghan, and remain numerous in the area. The MacDonnells of Antrim are in fact descendants of the Clan Donald. In the sixteenth century Somhairle Buidhe ('Sorley Boy') MacDonnell conquered a large part of that county and defended it tenaciously against Gaelic Irish and English intrusions. In 1620 his son, Randal MacSorley MacDonald, was created Earl of Antrim.

MACEVOY

MacEvoy (or MacAvoy) is the phonetic anglicisation of *Mac Fhíodhbhuidhe*, possibly from the Irish

MACDONNELL

MACEVOY

fiodhbhadhach, 'man of the woods'. The most prominent family of the name originally held power in the barony of Moygoish in modern Co. Westmeath, but migrated southwest, where they became one of the well-known 'Seven Septs of Leix', ruling over an area in the parishes of Mountrath and Raheen in Co. Laois. In the early

Dunluce Castle, Co. Antrim, standing on a great sea-eroded rock, was the stronghold of the MacDonnells in the sixteenth and seventeenth centuries.

seventeenth century the most important leaders of the family were forcibly transported to Co. Kerry, together with other members of the 'Seven Septs', but the surname remains numerous in the Laois/Westmeath region. In the north of the country, MacEvoy was used as an erroneous equivalent of *Mac Giolla Bhuidhe*, 'son of the fair-haired youth', a Donegal name usually anglicised as 'McIlwee' or 'MacKelvey', and of *Mac an Bheatha*, 'son of life' (MacVeigh), a surname common in the Armagh/Louth region.

Above: the arms of the MacGillycuddy family. Right: Ballymalis Castle, Co. Kerry, with, in the background, MacGillycuddy's Reeks, whose name records the former power of the family in the region.

MACGILLYCUDDY

The surname comes from the Irish *Mac Giolla Mochuda*, meaning 'son of the devotee of (St) Mochuda'. Its adoption was quite unusual. St Mochuda, a pet form of Cárthach, meaning 'loving', was the seventh-century founder of the important monastic settlement of Lismore, in Co. Waterford. He was a native of Kerry, and when his fellow Kerryman Ailinn O'Sullivan became bishop of the diocese of Lismore in the mid-thirteenth century, he initiated the practice of the O'Sullivans paying particular devotion to this saint. As a result, the practice grew up among one of the leading families of the O'Sullivans of using *Giolla Mochuda* as a kind of title. The first to use *Mac Giolla Mochuda* was Conor, who is recorded as having slain Donal O'Sullivan Beare in 1563. His family, descendants of Donal Mor O'Sullivan, the common ancestor of O'Sullivan Mor and O'Sullivan

Beare (*see* O'Sullivan), continued to be known as 'MacGillycuddy O'Sullivan' or 'MacGillycuddy alias O'Sullivan' well into the seventeenth century, when MacGillycuddy became established as a surname in its own right. Even at this point, less-well-off members of the family continued to be known as 'O'Sullivan' for quite some time.

The family controlled a large territory in the Kerry baronies of Magunihy and Dunkerron; the name of the great mountains in Dunkerron, MacGillycuddys Reeks, preserves the record of their ownership. Members of the family retained large estates in the area down to the twentieth century. Unlike many other families of the old Gaelic aristocracy, their line of descent remains clear down to the present day; the current holder of the title 'the MacGillycuddy of the Reeks', recognised as such by the Genealogical Office, is Richard Denis Wyer MacGillycuddy, now resident in France.

MACGOVERN

MACGOVERN

MacGovern is the phonetic anglicisation of *Mag Shamhradháin*, from a diminutive of *samradh*, 'summer'. The name is closely linked with the original homeland where it first arose; in the traditional genealogies, Shamhradhán, the eleventh-century individual from whom the surname comes, was himself descended from Eochaidh, one of the O'Rourkes, who lived in the eighth century. His name was given to the area of Co. Cavan where the MacGoverns held sway, the barony of Tullyhaw (*Teallach Eochaidh*), in the northwest of the county. The particular centres of their power were Bawnaboy, Lissanover, and Ballymagauran. This last includes an earlier anglicisation of *Mag Shamhradháin*, 'Magauran' or 'MacGowran', now much less common than MacGovern. From Cavan, the name has now spread throughout Connacht and Ulster, and is particularly numerous in the adjoining counties of Fermanagh and Leitrim.

MACGOWAN

MacGowan (or Magowan) is the phonetic anglicisation of the Irish *Mac Gabhann* and the Scottish *Mac Gobhann*, both meaning 'son of the smith'. In Ireland the surname originated in central Co. Cavan, in what was once the ancient kingdom of Breffny, where the MacGowans were among the most powerful families. However, in Cavan itself a large majority translated their surname and became Smiths (see also the entry for that name). Outside Cavan, in the adjoining counties of Leitrim, Donegal, Sligo and Monaghan, MacGowan was the most popular English form, and the surname is most numerous in those counties today, with the largest

number in Co. Donegal. There, a family of MacGowans held Church lands in the parish of Inishmacsaint. Because of their prominence, a separate Donegal family based near Raphoe, the *Mac Dhubháin* (from a diminutive of *dubh*, 'black') also anglicised their name as MacGowan, adding to the numbers bearing the name in that county.

MACGRATH

MacGrath, and its many variants: Magrath, MacGraw, Magra, comes from the Irish *Mac Raith*, from the personal name *Rath*, meaning 'grace' or 'prosperity'. Two native Irish families adopted the name, one based on the borders of the modern counties of Donegal and Fermanagh, around Termon MacGrath, the other in Co. Clare, where they were famous as hereditary poets to the ruling O'Brien family of Thomond. Today neither area can be claimed to have large numbers of the surname. The southern family spread eastwards, into counties Tipperary and Waterford, while the northern family's descendants are now mainly to be found in Co. Tyrone, where they settled around Ardstraw after being driven from their homeland by the O'Donnells. The most remarkable bearer of the name was of this family, Meiler Magrath (1523-1622), who managed to be, simultaneously, Catholic Bishop of Down and Connor and Protestant Archbishop of Cashel. His rapacity was notorious, and he held six Anglican bishoprics, four of them at the one time, as well as the income of seventy parishes. For his pains he lived to be a hundred years old.

MACGUINNESS

MacGuinness, together with its variants Guinness, Magennis, MacNeice, MacCreesh and others, comes from the Irish *Mac Aonghasa*, from the personal name Aonghas ('Angus'), made up of *aon* 'one' and *gus* 'choice', which was borne by a famous eighth-century Pictish king of Scotland, said to be a son of the Irish god Daghda, and Bóinn, the goddess who gave her name to the river Boyne. The surname originated in Iveagh, in what is now Co. Down, where the family displaced the O'Haugheys in the twelfth century, ruling over the region down to the seventeenth century. The centre of their power was at Rathfriland. In the sixteenth century

MACGRATH

MACGUINNESS

MACHUGH

they accepted the Reformation, but joined in the later wars against the English and were dispossessed of all their lands. The name is now common in Connacht and Leinster, as well as in its original homeland of Ulster

A southern offshoot of the family adopted the variant MacCreesh, and in Monaghan, Fermanagh and south Down that name was used as an equivalent of MacGuinness. North of the original homeland, in Co. Antrim, a similar process occurred, with MacNiece or MacNeice the variant adopted there. The Guinness family who founded the famous brewery were originally from Co. Down

MACHUGH

Along with its principal variant MacCue, MacHugh comes from the Irish *Mac Aodha* or *Aoidhe*, from the very popular personal name *Aodh*, meaning 'fire'. In various forms, *Aodh* is the root of a large number of common surnames (*see* Hayes, Hughes *and* Magee). At least three distinct families in west Ulster and Connacht adopted *Mac Aodha*: a branch of the O'Flahertys of Connemara in west Galway, another family based near the modern town of Tuam in north Galway and, in Fermanagh, a family who claim descent from Aodh, a grandson of Donn Carrach Maguire, the first Maguire ruler of the county. Today the surname is most numerous in Co. Donegal and in north Connacht, though it is also common in Leinster. In parts of Ulster – Fermanagh in particular – it was considered interchangeable with Magee until quite recently.

MACKENNA

MacKenna is the English form of the Irish surname *Mac Cionath*. The *Mac Cionath* were originally based in Meath, but in early times were brought north into Clogher as hired fighters by the rulers of that territory, and quickly became lords in their own right of Truagh, a territory on the borders of the modern counties of Tyrone and Monaghan. Their power endured down to the seventeenth century, their last chief being Patrick McKenna, who died near Emyvale, Co. Monaghan, in 1616. The surname is still very numerous in the area of the original homeland, but over the centuries has spread

MACKENNA

throughout the country. Juan MacKenna (1771-1814) was born at Clogher in Co. Tyrone and was a general under Bernardo O'Higgins in the fight for Chilean liberation.

MACKEON

MacKeon has a wide range of synonyms and variants, including Keon, MacKeown, MacGeown, MacOwen and, in Ulster, MacEwan, MacCune, MacKone, Magowen and, occasionally, Johnson or Johnstone. The reason lies in the Irish and Scottish original of the name, *Mac Eoin*, 'son of Eoin (John)', which arose independently in a number of areas. In Ireland the principal areas of origin were in the Kiltartan region of Co. Galway, at Creggan and Derrynoone in Co. Armagh and in Sligo/Leitrim in north Connacht. This last family were the most prominent historically, and it is thought that the Galway family were an offshoot. In Co. Antrim, the surname is almost entirely of Scottish origin, and derives from Eoin Bissett, who came to the Glens of Antrim from Scotland

in the thirteenth century. The form MacKeown is largely confined to northeast Ulster, while MacKeon is most common in Connacht and west Ulster. As so often with variations in spelling, however, no absolute rules are possible.

Donegal, where the family were among the most powerful in Ulster down to the late middle ages, and in Co. Meath, where the descendants of the tenth-century high king, Maolseachlann (or Malachy II), were first known as O'Melaghlin, later corrupted to MacLoughlin.

MACKEON

MACLOUGHLIN

MACLOUGHLIN

MacLoughlin is the form of the name most frequent in Connacht and Leinster, while McLaughlin is most common in Ulster, particularly in counties Antrim, Donegal and Derry. Both forms derive from the Irish and Scottish *Mac Lochlainn*, from the personal name Lochlann, from *loch*, 'lake' or 'fjord', and *lann*, meaning 'land'. It was a Gaelic name used for Scandinavia, and was applied to the Viking settlers of the early Middle Ages, and became a popular name in its own right. The surname containing it has at least three origins in Ireland: in Co. Clare, where the MacLoughlins claimed descent from Lochlann, a tenth-century lord in the barony of Corcomroe; in the Inishowen peninsula of Co.

MACMAHON

MacMahon (or MacMahon) comes from the Irish *Mac Mathghamha* or, in the modern version, *Mac Mathúna*, from *mathghamhqain*, meaning 'bear'. The surname arose separately in two areas, in west Clare and in Co. Monaghan. In the former, the MacMahons were part of the great tribal grouping, the *Dál gCais*, and claim decent from Mahon O'Brien, grandson of Brian Boru. The last Chief of the Name was killed at the battle of Kinsale in 1602. The Ulster MacMahons were based in the barony of Truagh in the north of Co. Monaghan, and ruled the kingdom of Oriel between the thirteenth and sixteenth centuries. Their last chief, Hugh MacMahon, was beheaded by the English in 1641. Today, although

MACMAHON

MACMANUS

the introduction of Magnus as a personal name, the surname it gave rise to is entirely Irish. It came into being in two distinct areas: in Co. Roscommon, where the family claim descent from Mághnais, son of the twelfth-century High King, Turlough O'Connor; and in Co. Fermanagh, where the original ancestor was Maghnuis Maguire, son of the chieftain Donn Mór

widespread throughout Ireland, MacMahon remains most common in the two ancestral homelands of Clare and Monaghan.

After the defeats of the native Irish in the seventeenth century, many of the Clare MacMahons emigrated to serve in the Irish Brigade of the French army. One of their descendants, Patrick MacMahon (1808-93), became President and Marshal of France.

MACMANUS

MacManus is the anglicisation of the Irish *Mac Mághnais*, from the popular Norse personal name Magnus, derived ultimately from the Latin *magnus*, 'great'. Although the Viking settlers are responsible for

Maguire. In Fermanagh they were second in power only to the Maguires themselves, and from their base on the island of Ballymaguire (now Belleisle) on Lough Erne controlled the shipping and fishing on the lake. Cathal Óg MacManus (1439-1498), chief of the name, dean of Lough Erne and vicar-general of the diocese of Clogher, was responsible for the compilation of the *Annals of Ulster*. Today the surname is most common by far in its original homelands, and especially in Co. Fermanagh.

MACNALLY

MacNally, MacAnally and Nally all share the same Irish origins, in the two Irish names *Mac an Fhailghigh*, 'son of the poor man', and *Mac Con Uladh*, 'son of the

MACNALLY

MACNAMARA

hound of Ulster'. As might be expected, the latter name is almost entirely confined to Ulster, in particular to that part of the modern province originally called *Ulaidh*, the southeast, in particular counties Armagh and Monaghan. Today, the anglicised versions of the name remain very common in these counties, with the 'Mac-' forms in the majority. Outside Ulster, the principal origin of the name is in northwest Connacht, in counties Roscommon and Mayo, where it is said that the name was adopted by the descendants of Norman settlers. The most common form in these counties is the simple 'Nally'. One extremely prominent bearer of the name was the Reverend David Rice MacAnally (1810-1895), a sheriff and Methodist preacher who is said to have weighed more than 360lbs (160kg).

MACNAMARA

MacNamara comes from the Irish *Mac Conmara*, 'son of the hound of the sea'. The surname arose in Co. Clare, where the family were part of the famous *Dál gCais* tribal grouping. They were second only to the O'Briens, to whom they were hereditary marshals. From relatively minor beginnings they grew in power to become rulers

of the territory of Clancullen, a territory including a large part of what is now east Clare, where they held sway for almost six centuries, down to the final defeat of Gaelic culture in the seventeenth century. Today, the surname is widespread throughout Ireland, but the largest concentration remains in the area of the original homeland, in counties Clare and Limerick. Brinsley MacNamara (1890-1963), the novelist and playwright, and the most famous modern bearer of the surname, was in fact John Weldon. He adopted the pseudonym as protection; his most famous work, *The Valley of the Squinting Windows*, was highly critical of Irish rural life.

MADDEN

Madden is is the anglicised version of the Irish *Ó Madaidhín*, from a diminutive of *madadh*, meaning 'hound'. In early times, the family were part of the *Uí Máine* tribal grouping based in east Co. Galway, and ruled the area up to the late Middle Ages. Even today, the surname is most numerous by far in east Galway. A branch of the family moved south to the Clare/Limerick region in early times, and anglicised their name as 'Madigan', and this separate surname is also still most

MADDEN   MAGUIRE

strongly associated with its original homeland. The most famous bearer of the name was Richard Robert Madden (1798-1886), doctor, traveller, historian and fervent opponent of the slave trade.

MAGEE

Magee, and its variants McGee, MacGee etc., come from the Gaelic *Mac* or *Mag Aodha*, from Aodh (anglicised 'Hugh'), a very popular personal name meaning 'fire', which also gave rise to a large number of other surnames, including Hays, Hughes, McHugh, and McCoy. The form 'Magee' reflects the pronunciation of Ulster and Scottish Gaelic, with 'Mag-' most common in the east of the province, and 'Mac-' in the west; Ulster is the area where the name is most common by far. It can be of either Scottish or Irish origin. Three Irish families of the name are recorded: in the area now on the borders of counties Donegal and Tyrone, in the territory around Islandmagee on the coast of Antrim, and in Fermanagh, where they descend from Aodh, great-grandson of Donn Carrach Maguire, the first Maguire

ruler of that region. The remainder of the Ulster Magees are descended from seventeenth-century settlers from Scotland, where the surname is most common in Dumfries, in Ayrshire and in Galloway. In Co. Cavan, *Mag Aodha* has also sometimes, strangely, been anglicised as 'Wynne', from a mistaken resemblance to *gaoth*, 'wind'.

MAGUIRE

Maguire, with its variants MacGuire, McGwire etc., comes from the Irish *Mag Uidhir*, meaning 'son of the brown(-haired) one'. The surname is now extremely common throughout Ireland, with particular concentrations in Cavan, Monaghan and Fermanagh; in Fermanagh it is the single most numerous name in the county. The reason is not far to seek. From the time of their first firm establishment, in Lisnaskea around the start of the thirteenth century, all the associations of the family have been with Fermanagh. By the start of the fourteenth century, the chief of the family, Donn Carrach Maguire, was ruler of the entire county, and for the

MAHER

meachar, meaning 'hospitable'. The surname originated in Ikerrin near the modern town of Roscrea in north Tipperary, where the family retained their traditional lands right up to the modern period. The name remains very strongly linked to the traditional homeland, with the bulk of present-day Mahers living or originating in Co. Tipperary. Thomas Francis Meagher (1823-1867) was one of the founders of the revolutionary 'Young Ireland' movement. Transported to Australia, he managed to escape to the U.S., where he became Brigadier-General of the Irish Brigade of the Union Army during the Civil War, and was later Governor of Montana.

MALONE

following three hundred years there were no fewer than fifteen Maguire chieftains of the territory. By the year 1600, Co. Fermanagh quite simply belonged to the family.

As for so many other Gaelic families, however, the seventeenth century was catastrophic for the Maguires. First, a junior branch, based around the area of the modern town of Enniskillen, were dispossessed and their lands parcelled out in the Plantation of Ulster. Then, as a result of their participation in the rebellions of the Cromwellian and Williamite periods, virtually all the remainder of their possessions in Fermanagh were taken.

Unlike the bulk of the native Irish aristocracy, the descent of the Maguires has remained intact. The current bearer of the title 'Maguire of Fermanagh' is Terence Maguire, officially recognised by the Chief Herald of Ireland in 1991 as the senior male descendant of the last inaugurated Maguire chief.

MAHER

Maher, and its principal variant Meagher, are the anglicised versions of the Irish *Ó Meachair*, from

MALONE

Malone is the anglicised form of the Irish *Ó Maoil Eoin*, meaning 'descendant of a devotee of (St) John', *maol* being the Irish for 'bald' and referring to the distinctive tonsure sported by Irish monks. The family was an offshoot of the O'Connors of Connacht, and lived up to the ecclesiastical origin of their surname in their long connection with the famous Abbey of Clonmacnoise, with a long line of Malone bishops and abbots. Today they are largely dispersed from this area, and the largest

MARTIN

Like many Irish surnames, Maher remains strongly associated with the area where it originated. The landscape of Tipperary has been familiar to thousands bearing the name Maher over the centuries.

concentrations are to be found in counties Clare and Wexford. The most famous bearer of the name was Edmund Malone (1741-1812), a friend of Samuel Johnson, James Boswell, and Edmund Burke amongst others, whose complete edition of the works of Shakespeare remained standard for almost a century.

MARTIN

Martin is an extremely common name throughout the English-speaking world and, in its many variant forms, throughout Europe; its popularity is largely due to the widespread fame of the fourth-century saint, Martin of Tours. In Ireland, the surname may be of English, Scottish or native Irish origin. The best-known Martins, powerful in west Galway and Galway city for centuries, were of English extraction, having arrived with the

MEEHAN

MOLLOY

Normans. The largest number of Irish origin stem from the *Mac Giolla Mhártain*, 'son of the follower of (St) Martin', also anglicised as 'Gilmartin', who were a branch of the O'Neills. They originally held territory in the barony of Clogher in Co. Tyrone, but were displaced westwards into the adjoining counties of Sligo and Leitrim, where they are most numerous today. The Scottish origin of the name is similar, from an anglicisation of Scots Gaelic *Mac Gille Mhártainn*. Richard ('Humanity Dick') Martin (1754-1834), of the Galway family, was one of the founders of the Royal Society for the Prevention of Cruelty to Animals.

MEEHAN

Meehan, along with its variant Meighan, comes from the Irish *O Miadhacháin*, from *miadhach*, meaning 'honourable'. Historically, the most notable family of the name were an offshoot of the MacCarthys of the kingdom of Desmond in south Munster. However, as early as the eleventh century they migrated north to Co.

Leitrim. From there they spread slowly into the adjoining counties, and are now numerous throughout east Connacht, Donegal and Fermanagh. This family preserved a sixth-century manuscript of St Molaise of Devenish from generation to generation for more than a thousand years; it is now held in the National Museum in Dublin. A separate family appears to have adopted the surname in the Clare/Galway region, where the name is also numerous. In Monaghan, and there alone, it has been anglicised as 'Meegan'.

MOLLOY

Molloy, along with Mulloy and O'Molloy, is the anglicised version of a number of distinct Irish names. The *Ó Maolmhuaidh*, from *maolmhuadh* meaning 'proud chieftain', were part of the southern *Uí Néill*, the southern branch of the large tribal grouping claiming descent from Niall of the Nine Hostages, the fifth-century king who supposedly kidnapped St Patrick to Ireland. They held power over a large part of what is

MOLONEY

now Co. Offaly, where the surname is still very common. A second family were the *Ó Maoil Aodha*, 'descendant of the devotee of (St) Aodh', from *maol*, literally 'bald', a reference to the distinctive tonsure sported by early Irish monks. As well as Molloy, this surname has also been anglicised as 'Miley' and 'Millea'. The name arose in east Connacht, in the Roscommon/east Galway region, and remains numerous there today.

MOLONEY

Moloney, along with its variants Mullowney and Maloney, is the English version of *Ó Maol Dhomhnaigh*, meaning 'descendant of the servant of the church', *Maol* means 'bald', and refers to the distinctive tonsure common in the early Irish Church, while *domhnach* means 'Sunday', and was used by extension to refer to the place of worship on that day. The surname arose in Co. Clare, near the modern town of Tulla, and remains extremely common there, as well as in the adjoining counties of Limerick and Tipperary. Mullowney has also sometimes been used as the anglicisation of the Ulster surname *Mac Giolla Dhomhnaigh*, meaning 'son of the servant of the church', usually anglicised as

'Downey' or 'MacEldowney', which is found principally in counties Antrim and Derry. Both of these name were sometimes used for the illegitimate offspring of clergymen.

MONAGHAN

Monaghan is the English version of the Irish *Ó Manacháin*, from a diminutive of *manach*, meaning 'monk', and some of the family adopted the semi-translation 'Monks'. Most of the surname in Ireland descend from one Manachain, a chieftain who lived in Connacht in the ninth century, and it is with that province, specifically with east Roscommon close to the river Shannon, that the family are most closely linked. Up to the end of the thirteenth century they were rulers of this area, known as 'the Three Tuathas'. The name has spread from the original homeland, and is now common also in Mayo and Galway. In Co. Fermanagh, where the name is also numerous, the family are thought to be part of the original inhabitants of the area, the Fir Manach, from whom the county gets its name. Their base was in the district of Lurg. From here the name has now also scattered in the adjoining counties of Monaghan and Derry.

MONAGHAN

MOONEY

MORAN

MOONEY

Mooney comes from the Irish *Ó Maonaigh*, which may derive from the Old Irish *maonach*, meaning 'dumb', or from *maoineach*, meaning 'wealthy'. It arose as a surname independently in each of the four provinces. In Ulster, it was the name of a family based in the parish of Ardara, in Co. Donegal. The Connacht family were located in the parish of Easky in the barony of Tireragh in Co. Sligo, where 'Meeny' is often the English version used. In Munster, reflecting the different pronunciation, the English is often 'Mainey'. But the most notable family arose in Leinster, in the modern Co. Offaly, where they were concentrated around the parish of Lemanaghan. Their descendants are by far the most numerous today, although the name has now spread throughout Ireland.

MOORE

Moore is today one of the most common surnames in Ireland, among the top twenty. It may be of English, Irish, Welsh or Scottish origin. In England the name may derive either from someone who lived near a moor or from a nickname for someone of dark complexion, from 'moor', meaning Negro. This is frequently also the ultimate origin of the name in Scotland and Wales, where it is often rendered 'Muir', although in places it is thought to come from *mór*, 'big'. The Irish origin of Moore is *Ó Mórdha*, also anglicised O'More, from *mórdha*, meaning 'stately' or 'noble'. The principal family of definite native Irish origin were of Co. Laois, where they were the leading sept of the famous 'Seven Septs of Laois', whose resistance to the English led to the forced resettlement of the most prominent individuals in Co. Kerry. At this point, it is virtually impossible to say in any single case which of the various origins of the surname is the most accurate.

MORAN

Moran is the anglicisation of two distinct Irish names, *Ó Móráin*, from *mór*, meaning 'big', and *Ó Mughráin*, whose origins remain unclear. The former arose in Co. Mayo, near the modern town of Ballina, where the eponymous ancestor Móran held power. The latter family were part of the *Uí Máine* tribal grouping. Their two branches were based around Criffon in Co. Galway, and the modern village of Ballintober in north Roscommon. Today, as might be expected, the vast majority of Morans are of Connacht origin. One of the most famous bearers of the name was Michael Moran (1794-1856), better known by his nickname of 'Zozimus', who was blinded in infancy and made his living on the streets of Dublin with his recitations and ballads. A monument to him stands in Glasnevin cemetery.

MORGAN

In origin Morgan is Welsh, deriving from the Old Welsh *morcant,* meaning 'sea-bright'. The majority of Irish Morgans are almost certainly of Welsh or Welsh Norman stock. The surname is common in Connacht and Leinster, but most numerous in Ulster. Here, it is possible that some are descended from the Clann Morgunn of Sutherland in Scotland, or from a separate family based in Aberdeenshire. There is also a Gaelic Irish family in Ulster, the *Ó Murcháin*, who were based in Co. Monaghan, whose surname was anglicised Morgan. The writer Lady Sydney Morgan (1783-1859) had immense success with her books on the politics and society of France and Italy, and her salon in Kildare Street was the centre of Dublin literary life.

MORIARTY

Moriarty is the English version of the Irish *Ó Muircheartaigh*, made up of *muir*, 'sea', and *ceardach*, 'skilled', thus 'one skilled in the ways of the sea'. The name is undoubtedly linked to their original homeland, on both sides of Castlemaine harbour in south Co. Kerry. The continuity of their association with the area is remarkable, even by Irish standards. They have lived in the area since the surname came into being in the eleventh century, and ninety per cent of present births of the surname are still in Co. Kerry. This continuity is all the more tenacious for the fact that they had lost virtually all their power in the area by the fourteenth century. David Moriarty (1814-1877) was a Catholic bishop of Kerry notorious for his vehement denunciations of all opposition to the British government, saying of the Fenian leaders 'eternity is not

MORIARTY

MORRIS

long enough nor Hell hot enough for such miscreants.'
Ó Muircheartaigh was also a surname found in Meath
and the midlands, but in these areas it has been anglicised
as 'Murtagh'.

MORRIS

Morris is a common surname throughout the British
Isles, and in virtually all cases is derived, directly or
indirectly, from the personal name Maurice, which
comes from the Latin *Maurus*, meaning 'moorish' (*see*
Moore). A large number of those bearing the name in
Ireland, where the name is most frequent in Leinster,
with significant numbers also in Ulster and Connacht,
will be of English, Scottish or Welsh origin. There was

The landscape of Co. Sligo, with its rich intermingling of
bare mountains, lush countryside and wild sea, was
familiar territory to the *Ó Muirgheasa* family in times
gone by.

also an Irish family, the *Ó Muirgheasa*, (from *muir*, 'sea'
and *geasa*, 'taboo') part of the *Uí Fiachrach* tribal
grouping in Co. Sligo, whose surname was originally
anglicised Morrissey and later shortened to Morris. *Ó
Muirgheasa* was also the surname of a family in Co.
Fermanagh who anglicised their name to Morris. The
most prominent family of the name, one of the famous
'Tribes of Galway', were of Norman extraction and
originally known as de Marreis.

MULLAN

MULLAN

Mullan, together with its variants Mullin, Mullen, Mullane and Mullins, can have a variety of distinct origins. First, it may be the anglicisation of the Irish name *Ó Maoláin*, from a diminutive of *maol*, 'bald' or 'tonsured', which arose separately in a number of areas. The Co. Galway family of the name claim descent from Maolan, himself descended from a king of Connacht. A different family of the same name were based in the Keenaght district of Co. Derry, and were followers of the O'Cahans (*see* Kane). In Co. Monaghan a family of the name arose around the modern town of Clones; their name has also been anglicised as Mollins. Yet another family hails from south Co. Cork, where the name is frequently given as Mullins. As well as all of these, many MacMillans, Scottish settlers in Ulster in the seventeenth century, adopted MacMullan, often shortened to Mullan. There is also an English name Mullins, from the Middle English *miln*, 'mill', and a good number of Irish bearers of the name are undoubtedly of this origin.

MULLIGAN

Mulligan comes from the Irish *Ó Maolagáin*, from a diminutive of *maol*, literally meaning 'bald' and referring

to the distinctive tonsure of the early Irish monks. In the early Middle Ages they were rulers of the territory of *Tír MacCartháin*, in the baronies of Boylagh and Raphoe in Co. Donegal, and held power down to the plantation of the seventeenth century. After this they were dispersed, and migrated south to Mayo and east to counties Fermanagh and Monaghan. Some members of the family anglicised their surname, by quasi-translation, to Baldwin. Milligan is another common variant, found most frequently in counties Antrim, Down and Derry. Hercules Mulligan (1740-1825), born in Coleraine, acted as a secret agent for George Washington during the War of Independence.

MURPHY

Murphy is the anglicised version of two Irish surnames, *Ó Murchadha* and *Mac Murchadha*, both derived from the popular early Irish personal name *Murchadh*, meaning 'sea-warrior'. *Mac Murchadha* ('son of *Murchadh*') is exclusive to Ulster, where the family were part of the *Cinéal Eoghain*, the tribal grouping claiming descent from Eoghan, himself a son of the fifth century founder of the *Uí Néill* dynasty, Niall of the Nine Hostages, who was reputedly responsible for the kidnapping of St Patrick to Ireland. These Ulster Murphys (or MacMuphys) were originally based in present-day

It has been claimed that the Murphys are 'even more Irish than those who are more Irish than the Irish themselves.'

MURPHY

Co. Tyrone, in the area known as *Muintir Birn*, but were driven out by the O'Neills and settled in south Armagh, where they were subjects of the O'Neills of the Fews. In Ulster today, Murphy remains most numerous in Co. Armagh, though it is also to be found in great numbers in Fermanagh and Monaghan

Elsewhere in Ireland, *O Murchadha* (descendant of *Murchadh*) is the original Irish. This arose separately in at least three distinct areas: in Cork, Roscommon and Wexford. The most prominent of these were the Wexford *Uí Murchadha*. These took their surname from *Murchadh*

or Murrough, grandfather of Dermot MacMurrough, King of Leinster, and thus share their origin not only with the MacMurroughs but also with the Kinsellas, the Kavanaghs and the MacDavy Mores. Their territory lay in the barony of Ballaghkeen in Wexford, and was formerly known as Hy Felimy, from Felim, one of the sons of Éanna Cinsealaigh, the semi-legendary, fourth-century ruler of Leinster. Their chief seats in this area were at Morriscastle ('O Murchu's Castle'), Toberlamina, Oulart and Oularteigh. The last chief of the name to be elected by the old Gaelic method of tanistry was Murtagh, who in 1461 was granted the right to use English law, thus entitling him to pass on his possessions to his direct descendants. The arrangement lasted only until the late sixteenth century, when Dónal Mór O'Morchoe (as the name was then anglicised) was overthrown, and virtually all his territory confiscated; most of his followers were scattered and settled in the surrounding counties, in Kilkenny and Carlow particularly. One branch, however, based at Oularteigh, did manage to retain their lands, and their succession continues unbroken down to the present. David O'Morchoe (this version of the name was adopted by deed poll by his grandfather in 1895) is the current Chief of the Name, recognised as such by the Chief Herald of Ireland. The arms illustrated are for this family.

MURRAY

Murray is an extremely common surname throughout Ireland, among the twenty most numerous. It can be of Scottish or Irish origin. The Scottish surname, Murray or MacMurray, derives from Moray in the northeast of the country, a name which originally meant 'settlement by the sea'. The earliest recorded ancestor of this family was one Hugh Freskin, a Flemish settler who obtained large grants of land in Morayshire in 1130; his descendants took their name from his property. Many in Ireland, in Ulster particularly, are of this connection. In Ireland the surname came from *Ó Muireachaidh*, 'descendant of the seaman'. The most prominent family of the name were based in the south Roscommon/east Galway region, and were part of the *Uí Máine* tribal grouping. As well as these, however, a separate family of the same name are recorded in Cork, in the barony of Carbery, and *Mac Muireachaidh*, anglicised as Murray and MacMorrow, is found in Co. Leitrim and north Co. Down. In addition *Mac Giolla Mhuire*, 'son of the servant of Mary', another Co. Down name, has sometimes been anglicised as Murray, as well as the more obvious MacIlmurray and Gilmore.

NOLAN

Nolan is now among the most common surnames in Ireland. It is the anglicised form of *Ó Nualláin*, from a diminutive of *nuall*, meaning 'famous' or 'noble'. The

NOLAN

family are strongly linked with the area of the modern Co. Carlow, where in pre-Norman times they held power in the barony of Forth, whence their ancient title of 'Princes of Foharta'. Their power was greatly diminished after the arrival of the Normans, but the surname is still strongly linked with the area. The prevalence of the surname in the modern counties of Mayo and Galway is explained by the migration of a branch of the family to that area in the sixteenth century; they obtained large tracts of land, and their descendants are many. The most famous modern bearer of the surname was Brian O'Nolan (1911-1966), better known under his two pen-names of Flann O'Brien and Myles na Gopaleen, whose genius for comic invention has only been fully appreciated since his death.

O'BRIEN

O'Brien is in Irish *Ó Briain*, from the personal name Brian. The meaning of this is problematic. It may come from *bran*, meaning 'raven', or, more likely, from *Brion*,

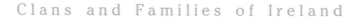

a borrowing from the Celtic ancestor of Welsh which contains the element *bre-*, meaning 'hill' or 'high place'. By association, the name would then mean 'lofty' or 'eminent'.

Whatever the initial meaning of the word, the historic origin of the surname containing it is clear. It simply denotes a descendant of Brian Boru, ('Brian of the Tributes'), High King of Ireland in 1002, and victor at the battle of Clontarf in 1014. He was a member of the relatively obscure *Uí Toirdealbhaigh*, part of the *Dál gCais* tribal grouping based in the Clare/Limerick area. Having secured control of the *Dál gCais* in 976, he defeated and killed the *Eoghanacht* king of Munster two

The Cliffs of Moher, on the coast of Co. Clare, the original home of Brian Boru, direct ancestor of the modern O'Briens. In the distance is the 'O'Brien Tower'.

years later, and proceeded to wage deadly war against the kingdoms of Connacht, Meath, Leinster and Breifne. Eventually he secured submission (and tributes) from all but the northern *Uí Néill*, the Leinstermen and the Vikings. His victory at Clontarf united all of Ireland, nominally at least, under a single leader, though Brian himself was slain.

O'BRIEN

The first individual clearly to use O'Brien as a genuinely hereditary surname was Donogh Cairbre O'Brien, son of the king of Munster, Dónal Mór. His descendants spilt into a number of branches, including the O'Briens of Aherlow, the O'Briens of Waterford, the O'Briens of Arra in north Tipperary, and the O'Briens of Limerick, where the surname is perpetuated in the name of the barony of Pubblebrien. Today the name is numerous and widespread throughout Ireland, with particular concentrations in these areas, as well as in the original homeland of Clare.

The surname has been prominent in all spheres of Irish life. The novelist and dramatist Kate O'Brien (1897-1954) suffered, like most Irish novelists of worth, at the hands of the censors in the early years of the Irish Free State. William Smith O'Brien (1803-1864) was one of the founders of the Young Ireland movement, and took a prominent part in the rising of 1848. His grandson Dermod O'Brien (1865-1945) was a leading portrait painter in Dublin for almost forty years.

O'CALLAGHAN

O'Callaghan, along with its variants (O')Callagan, Callahan etc., comes from the Irish *Ó Ceallacháin*, from the personal name Ceallachán, a diminutive of *ceallach*. This was traditionally taken to mean 'frequenter of churches', but is now thought to be a much older word meaning 'bright-headed'. The personal name was much in favour among the *Eoghanacht*, the tribal grouping who controlled the kingship of Munster before the rise of Brian Boru of the *Dál gCais*, and it is from one of the *Eoghanacht* kings, Ceallachán (d.954), that the family trace their descent. Murchadh Ua Ceallacháin, a grandson of this king who lived in the early eleventh century, was the first to transit the surname hereditarily.

Bunratty Castle was originally constructed in the fifteenth century by the MacNamaras, but was soon appropriated by the O'Briens, later Earls of Thomond. The modern restoration is thoroughly authentic.

O'CALLAGHAN

His nephew Cárthach was the ancestor of the MacCarthys, and a bloody succession feud between the MacCarthys and the O'Callaghans continued well into the twelfth century, ending with the MacCarthys in the ascendant.

By the end of the thirteenth century the O'Callaghans had taken decisive possession of that part of Co. Cork which came to be known as *Pobal Uí Cheallacháin*, O'Callaghan's Country. This was a very large area on both sides of the river Blackwater west of the modern town of Mallow. Here their principal bases were the castles at Clonmeen and Dromaneen, and from them they retained virtually uninterrupted control for over four centuries, continuing many of the earlier Gaelic customs. The most notorious of these was the *creach* or cattle-raid; one Donncha, chief of the family from 1537 until his undeservedly peaceful death in 1578, was reputed to have carried out two hundred raids in every county of Munster, evidently regarding the *creach* as a vital part of his cultural inheritance.

In the great confiscations following the wars of the seventeenth century the family lost virtually everything. The ruling chief, Donncha O'Callaghan, and his extended family were transplanted to east Clare, where they obtained land in the barony of Tulla. The village of O'Callaghan's Mills records their continued presence.

Like so many others from the old Gaelic aristocracy, members of this Clare family emigrated to continental Europe. Cornelius O'Callaghan entered the army of Spain in 1717. In 1944 one of his descendants, Don Juan O'Callaghan of Tortosa, was recognised by the Genealogical Office as the senior descendant in the male line of the last inaugurated chief, the Donncha who was transplanted to Clare.

O'CONNELL

O'Connell, along with Connell, generally comes from the Irish *Ó Conaill*, 'descendant of Conall', a very popular personal name probably derived from *con*, 'hound' and *gal*, 'valour'. Because of the widespread popularity of the personal name at its root, O'Connell arose separately as a surname in Connacht, Ulster and Munster. However, by far the most prominent and numerous of these were the O'Connells of Munster, where the family were originally lords of the barony of Magunihy in east Kerry.

O'CONNELL

The Dublin house at 70 Merrion Square, where Daniel O'Connell lived and worked as a barrister, is now the headquarters of the Irish Arts Council.

Driven from this area by the O'Donoghues, they moved south and the centre of their power shifted to Ballycarbery, also in Co. Kerry. Today a large majority of the O'Connells in Ireland are still to be found in Co. Kerry, as well as in adjoining Co. Cork. This family

produced the most famous bearer of the name, Daniel O'Connell (1775-1847), known as 'the Liberator' because he won Catholics the right to vote; for almost thirty years he was the undisputed leader of Catholic Ireland.

In Ulster, especially in counties Antrim, Tyrone and Down, many Connells and MacConnells are of Scottish stock, their names derived from a phonetic transliteration of *Mac Dhomhnaill*, since the 'Dh-' is not pronounced. This family were a branch of the great Clan Donald.

O'CONNOR

O'Connor, with its variants Connor, Conner, Connors etc., comes from the Irish *Conchobhair*, from the personal name Conchobhar, perhaps meaning 'lover of hounds' or 'wolf-lover'. This was one of the most favoured of early Irish names, and gave rise to the surname in at least five distinct areas, in Connacht (O'Conor Don), in Offaly (O'Conor Faly), in north Clare (O'Conor of Corcomroe), in Keenaght in Co. Derry, and in Kerry (O'Connor Kerry).

The Offaly family take their name from Conchobhar (d.979), who claimed descent from Cathaoir Mór, a second-century king of Ireland. They remained powerful in their original homeland until the sixteenth century, when they were dispossessed of their lands.

The O'Connor Kerry were chiefs of a large territory in north Kerry, displaced further northwards by the Norman invasion to the Limerick borders, where they retained much of their power down to the seventeenth century. Today, the descendants of these O'Connors are far and away the most numerous, with the majority of all the many O'Connors in Ireland concentrated in the Kerry/Limerick/Cork area.

However, the most famous of all the O'Connor families is that which arose in Connacht. The ancestor

Connor Pass, on the Dingle Peninsula in Kerry, one of the counties in which the surname O'Connor arose. Love of the land is an intensely Irish characteristic – the land is easy to love.

O'CONNOR   O'DONNELL

from whom they take their surname was Conchobhar, King of Connacht (d.971), and direct ancestor of the last two High Kings of Ireland, Turlough O'Connor and Roderick O'Connor, who ruled through the twelfth century. Unlike the vast majority of the rest of the old Gaelic aristocracy, the O'Conors of Connacht managed to retain a large measure of their property and influence through all the calamities from the seventeenth century on. The line of descent from the last Chief of the Name is also intact; the current 'O Conor Don', recognised as such by the Chief Herald of Ireland, is Denis O Conor. The family seat remains in the ancestral homeland, in Castlerea, Co. Roscommon.

O'DONNELL

O'Donnell comes from the Irish *O Domhnaill*, 'descendant of Domhnall', a name meaning 'world-mighty'. Given the popularity of this name, it is not surprising that the surname containing it arose simultaneously in a number of areas, among them west Clare and east Galway, where they were part of the *Uí*

Máine, the sept grouping under the control of the O'Kellys. The most famous O'Donnells, however, are undoubtedly those based in Donegal.

Like many northern families, the O'Donnells of Tír Chonaill were part of the great *Uí Néill* tribal grouping, claiming common descent from Niall of the Nine Hostages, the fifth-century monarch who is reputed to have kidnapped St Patrick to Ireland. They were not prominent in early times, inhabiting a relatively small territory around Kilmacrenan. From the late Middle Ages, however, their power and influence grew steadily until, by the fourteenth century, they were undisputed lords of Tír Chonaill, roughly identical to modern Co. Donegal.

Their dynasty continued for more than three centuries, culminating with their involvement in the Nine Years War, in which Red Hugh O'Donnell (1571-1602) and his brother Rory, First Earl of Tyrconnell (1575-1608), played a famous part, almost inflicting a decisive reverse on the progress of English rule. The defeat suffered by the alliance of the remaining pre-eminent Gaelic families was the beginning of the end for the old order in Ireland. Rory O'Donnell was one of

O'DONOGHUE

which derives from the popular personal name Donncha, from *donn*, meaning 'brown'. The surname would thus mean literally 'descendant of the brown-haired (or brown-complexioned) man'. The popularity of the personal name meant that the surname arose independently in a number of places, including Galway/Roscommon, Cork, Tipperary and Cavan. The anglicised versions vary slightly, with 'Donohoe' more common in Galway and Cavan.

The most important of these families historically speaking were the O'Donoghue of Desmond, or south Munster. These were part of the *Eoghanacht* peoples, dominant throughout the south of the country until the rise of the *Dál gCais* under Brian Boru, and shared their ancestry with the O'Mahonys. Like the O'Mahonys, the Desmond O'Donoghues saw their power greatly diminished by the steady rise of the MacCarthys. Ultimately they were completely displaced from their original homeland in west Cork, and settled in southwest Kerry. Here they split into two major groupings, the O'Donoghue Mór, based around Lough Leane near Killarney, and O'Donoghue of the Glen, based in Glenflesk.

O'Donoghue Mór shared the fate of the majority of the old Gaelic aristocracy, dispossession and poverty, but the O'Donoghue of the Glen managed to retain both the family property and the unbroken succession to the title through all the vicissitudes of the last four centuries. Geoffrey O Donoghue is the current bearer of the title O Donoghue of the Glens, recognised as Chief of his Name by the Chief Herald of Ireland.

Among the many bearers of the name are Juan O'Donoju (1751-1821), the last Spanish ruler of Mexico, descendant of an O'Donoghue emigrant to Spain; John O'Donoghue (1900-1964), a novelist who wrote movingly and simply about his experience of rural Ireland, and David James O'Donoghue (1866-1917) poet, librarian and man of letters.

those who took part in the 'Flight of the Earls', the departure from Lough Swilly in Donegal in 1607 of the most powerful remaining Irish leaders.

Unlike many others among the old Irish aristocracy, however, the line of their descent remains unbroken. The last duly inaugurated chief was Niall Garbh ('Rough'), and a direct line of succession from his younger brother Hugh Buidh ('Yellow') continues down to the present. The present 'O Donnell of Tirconnell', recognised as such by the Chief Herald of Ireland, is Aodh O Donnell, now living in Dublin.

O'DONOGHUE

(O')Donoghue, with its variants Donohue, Donahoe, Donohoe etc., comes from the Irish *Ó Donnchadha*,

O'DONOVAN

O'Donovan comes from the Irish *ÓDonndubháin*, from *donn*, 'brown' and *dubh*, 'black' or 'dark', the surname thus meaning 'descendant of the dark brown (-haired/complexioned) man'. the original Donnduban from whom the surname derives was king of *Uí Chairpre* in

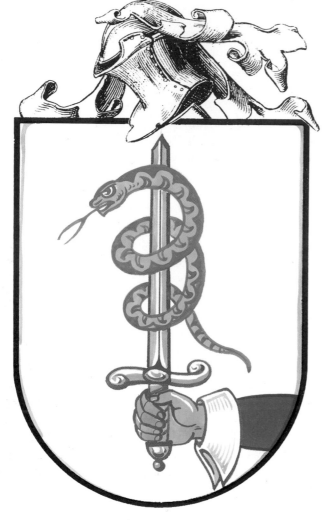

O'DONOVAN

but Colonel Daniel O'Donovan, the head of the family at that time, managed to regain some property in the area after the Treaty of Limerick, and re-established the family seat at Bawnlahan in the parishes of Myross and Castlehaven. From him descends the current Chief of the Name, Daniel O'Donovan of Hollybrook, Skibbereen, Co. Cork, the O'Donovan, recognised as such by the Chief Herald of Ireland.

The most famous bearer of the name was John O'Donovan (1809-1861), founder of the Irish Archaeological Society, who virtually single-handedly laid the foundation for all subsequent study of Irish genealogy, history, language and topography.

O'GRADY

O'Grady, along with Grady, comes from the Irish *Ó Grádaigh*, from *grádach*, meaning 'noble'. The surname originated in Co. Clare, where the *Ó Grádaigh* were part of the *Dál gCais* tribal grouping who claimed descent from Cas, a son of Oiloll Ollum, the semi-legendary third-century king of Munster. They thus shared common ancestry with the pre-eminent family of the *Dál gCais*, the O'Briens, and took a prominent part in the O'Briens' struggle against the rival *Eoghanacht* MacCarthys, descended from Eoghan, another son of Oiloll Ollum.

Although Clare was their homeland, from a very early date the family had strong associations with Co. Limerick, in particular the area around Kilballyowen. This was acquired by the then head of the family, Hugh O'Grady, in 1309, and has remained the principal seat of the family down to the present day. Unlike so many others of the native aristocracy, the O'Gradys sided with the English in the sixteenth century, and intermarried with a number of powerful English families, thus retaining their influence and possessions through all the vicissitudes of the seventeenth and eighteenth centuries. Two of those marriages, that of Darby O'Grady to Faith, daughter of Sir Thomas Standish of Lancaster in 1633, and of John O'Grady to Mary Elizabeth de Courcy, daughter of Baron Kinsale, are reflected to this day in the personal names in use in the family; the present O'Grady of Kilballyowen, popularly 'the O'Grady', and recognised as such by the Chief Herald of Ireland, is Gerald de Courcy O Grady.

what is now east Limerick, and died in 980. In the late twelfth century, as a result of the vicious struggle between the MacCarthys and the O'Briens for dominance in Munster, the O'Donovans were forced to migrate into the neighbouring county of Cork. There they gave the name of their kingdom to the modern barony of Carbery. Their territory comprised a large portion of this area reaching from the southeast coast almost as far as the modern town of Bantry. Their principal seat was at Castledonovan, in the centre of Drimoleague parish.

The family remained powerful and prominent in the area down to the seventeenth century, when they played an important role in the defence of the Catholic and Gaelic Irish against the Cromwellian and Williamite campaigns. Like so many other members of the native aristocracy, the chiefs of the family were dispossessed in the punitive confiscations of the end of that century,

O'HARA

O'KEEFFE

The most prominent historical bearers of the name were Standish Hayes O'Grady (1832-1915) and his cousin Standish James O'Grady (1846-1928). Both were deeply involved in the nineteenth-century revival of interest in the Gaelic past of Ireland, the former as a renowned scholar and student of early Irish history and society, the latter as a popular novelist who based his stories on Irish legends and history.

O'HARA

O'Hara is a phonetic anglicisation of *Ó hEaghra*. The family claim descent from *Eaghra*, lord of Luighne (the modern Leyney) in Co. Sligo, who died in 976 and who was himself, in the traditional genealogies, of the family of Oiloll Ollum, king of Munster. The O'Haras remain strongly associated with Co. Sligo, where they were chiefs in two areas, *Ó hEaghra Buidhe* ('fair') around Collooney, and *Ó hEaghra Riabhach* ('grey') at Ballyharry, more properly 'Ballyhara'. In the fourteenth century a branch of the family migrated north to the Glens of Antrim and established themselves in the area around the modern town of Ballymena. There they intermarried with powerful local families and acquired great prominence themselves. Apart from Dublin, Sligo and Antrim are still the two regions where the surname is most concentrated.

O'KEEFFE

O'Keeffe, and Keeffe, are the anglicised versions of the Irish *Ó Caoimh*, from *caomh*, meaning 'kind' or 'gentle'. The original *Caomh* from whom the family descend lived in the early eleventh century, and was a descendant of Art, King of Munster from 742 to 762. Originally the territory of the family lay along the banks of the Blackwater river in Cork, but the arrival of the Normans displaced them, like so many others, and they moved west into the barony of Duhallow, where their territory became known, and is still known, as Pobal O'Keeffe. The chiefs of the family retained power down to the eighteenth century, despite their involvement in the various rebellions, but were eventually dispossessed. Even today, Pobal O'Keeffe is still the area in which the name is most common, with surrounding areas of Co. Cork also including many of the name. It remains relatively rare outside that county.

O'MAHONY

O'NEILL

these areas they retained a large measure of power and wealth until the final collapse of Gaelic power in the wars of the seventeenth century. The most famous modern bearer of the name was Eoin ('the Pope') O'Mahony (1904-1970), barrister and genealogist, who

O'MAHONY

O'Mahony, the most common contemporary form of the name, comes from the Irish *Ó Mathghamhna*, stemming, like MacMahon, from *mathghamhan*, meaning 'bear'. The surname was adopted in the eleventh century by one of the dominant families of the Munster *Eoghanacht* peoples, the *Cinéal Aodha*; the individual from whom the name derives was the child of a marriage between Cian, chief of the *Cinéal Aodha*, and Sadhbh, daughter of Brian Boru. With the rise of the MacCarthys in the twelfth century the influence of the O'Mahonys declined, and was largely confined to the two areas of west Cork with which they are still most strongly associated, the Iveagh peninsula and the barony of Kinalmeaky, around the modern town of Bandon. In

preserved and interpreted with accuracy and enthusiasm the traditions of his own and many other families, founding and organizing the annual clan gathering of the O'Mahonys.

O'NEILL

O'Neill is in Irish *Ó Néill*, from the personal name Niall, possibly meaning 'passionate' or 'vehement'. A clear distinction needs to be kept in mind between the family bearing this surname and the *Uí Néill*, the powerful tribal grouping claiming descent from Naill of the Nine Hostages, the fifth century monarch supposedly responsible for kidnapping St. Patrick to Ireland. Out of the *Uí Néill* came many other well-known surnames,

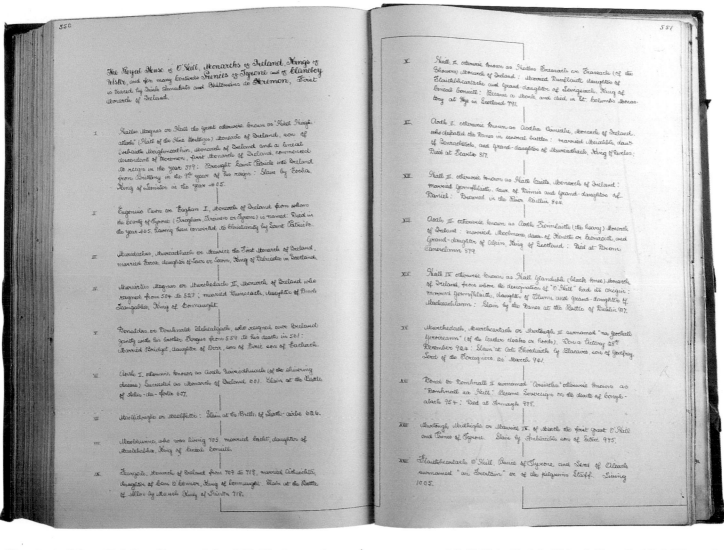

The start of the official pedigree of the O'Neills, housed at the Genealogical Office in Dublin, is a reminder that the family can justly claim to be one of the most ancient in Europe.

including O'Doherty, O'Donnell, O'Hagan and others. Within the *Uí Néill* the two principal sub-groups were the *Cinéal Eoghain* and the *Cinéal Cónaill*, claiming descent from two of the sons of Niall, Eoghan and Conall respectively. The O'Neills were the leading family of the *Cinéal Eoghain*, ruling the ancient territory of *Tír Eoghain*, comprising not only the modern Co. Tyrone, but also large parts of Derry and Donegal. The first to use the name in recognizable hereditary fashion was Donal, born *c*.943; the individual on whom he based his

name was *Niall Glún Dubh* ('Black Knee'), High King of Ireland who died in 919.

In the fourteenth century a branch of the *Tír Eoghain* O'Neills migrated eastwards and, under the leadership of Aodh Buidhe ('Yellow Hugh'), wrested large areas of Antrim and Down from Norman control. The territory at the centre of their power, Clandeboy, took its name from them (*Clann Aodha Buidhe*), and they in turn became known as the Clandeboy O'Neills. Their principal castle was at Edenduffcarrig, northwest of Antrim town, still occupied by an O'Neill. The present titular head of this branch of the family is Hugo O'Neill, 'O'Neill of Clandeboy', a Portuguese businessman descended from Muircheartach, chief of the family from 1548 to 1552.

The descent of the original Tyrone family has also continued unbroken, down to the present holder of the

title of *Ó Néill Mór*, Don Carlos O'Neill of Seville, who also holds the Spanish titles of Marqués de la Granja, Marqués del Norte and Conde de Banajir. He is descended, through the O'Neills of the Fews in Co. Armagh, from Aodh, second son of Eoghan, inaugurated as chief of the name in 1432.

O'ROURKE

O'Rourke comes from the Irish *Ó Ruairc,* from Ruarc, a personal name derived from the Old Norse *Hrothekr* (whence also 'Roderick'), meaning 'famous king'. Further Viking influence is seen in the frequency in the family of such names as Lochlann, Amhlaoibh (Olaf) and Sitric.

The O'Rourkes were of the same stock as the O'Connors of Connacht, part of the large tribal grouping of the *Uí Briain*, claiming common descent from Brion, a fifth-century King of Connacht. In the early Middle Ages, the O'Connors and the O'Rourkes were engaged in a long and bloody struggle for supremacy in Connacht, a struggle which ended in the victory of the O'Connors.

The Ruarc from whom the surname derives was a ninth-century King of Breifne, an area covering most of the modern counties of Leitrim and Cavan, along with part of Co. Longford. The first to use his name as part of an hereditary surname was his grandson, Seán Fearghal Ó Ruairc, who died in 964. Over the following century and a half, four O'Rourkes were Kings of Connacht. After the twelfth century, they appear to have accepted the overlordship of the O'Connors, however reluctantly. They also had persistent problems with the other pre-eminent family of Breifne, the O'Reillys, which ultimately resulted in their territory being much reduced. The main stronghold of the family was at Dromahair, on the shores of Lough Gill in Co. Leitrim.

In common with most of the other ruling families of Gaelic Ireland, the O'Rourkes lost all of their possessions in the great upheavals of the sixteenth and seventeenth centuries. However, the line of descent from the last Chief of the Name, Brian Ballagh O'Rourke, who was inaugurated in 1529 and died in 1562, remains intact. The present holder of the title 'O Ruairc of Breifne', recognised as Chief of his Name by the Chief Herald of Ireland is Philip O Rorke, resident in London.

O'ROURKE

O'SULLIVAN

O'SHEA

O'SHEA

O'Shea, Shea and (O')Shee are anglicisations of the Irish *Ó Séaghdha*, from the personal name *Séaghdha*, meaning either 'hawk-like' or 'fortunate'. The surname arose in south Kerry, on the Iveragh peninsula, where the family held power in the early Middle Ages. Despite the later decline in their influence, they were not displaced, remaining extremely numerous in their original homeland down to the present day. The surname is also found in some numbers in counties Tipperary and Kilkenny. These are the descendants of family members who migrated north as early as the fourteenth century. They became prominent in Kilkenny especially, where the name was more often anglicised (O')Shee. The most famous bearer of the name in Irish history was Katharine O'Shea, mistress and later wife of Charles Stewart Parnell; their love affair brought about Parnell's downfall and changed the course of Irish history.

O'SULLIVAN

The original Irish is *Ó Súileabháin*, deriving from *súil* (eye). The dispute over the meaning of the remainder of the name is understandable, since the two principal

alternatives are 'one-eyed' or 'hawk-eyed'. In Irish mythology, they are part of the Eoghanacht tribal grouping, descended, along with such prominent families as the MacCarthys and O'Callaghans, from the mythical Eoghan, supposedly one of the original Gaelic invaders. In historical times the O'Sullivans split into two major branches, the O'Sullivan Mór, based on the shores of Kenmare Bay in Co. Kerry, and the O'Sullivan Beare, around Bantry and the Beara peninsula in Co. Cork. Cork and Kerry are the areas in which popular tradition places the earliest Gaelic settlements, and even today, four out of five families of the name still live in the two counties, where it is the single most common surname.

The brass crest associated with the arms of O'Sullivan Beare, depicting a robin standing on a lizard's back.

O'TOOLE

O'Toole, along with Toole, comes from the Irish *Ó Tuathail*. This derives from the personal name Tuathal, meaning 'ruler of the people', used by many Irish kings and heroes and accordingly incorporated into a surname in a number of distinct areas, among them south Ulster, Mayo and Kildare. Today the vast majority of those bearing the name are descended from the Kildare O'Tooles. The individual from whom the surname is taken was Tuathal, King of Leinster, who died *c*.958; the first to use the surname in true hereditary fashion

The falls at Glen Macnass, near Laragh in Co. Wicklow.
Despite its proximity to Dublin, the centre of English
power in Ireland from the Middle Ages, Wicklow
remained unconquered until the seventeenth century.
This was partly due to the wild terrain, but the fierce
independence of such powerful families as the O'Byrnes
and the O'Tooles was legendary.

appears to have been his grandson Doncaon, slain at
Leighlin in 1014.

Although the original territory of the O'Tooles lay in
Co. Kildare, in the twelfth century they were displaced
by the invading Normans and migrated into the adjoining
county of Wicklow, where the area they controlled was
roughly identical to the old diocese of Glendalough,
with the centre of their power in the region around the
Glen of Imaal. Despite the proximity of Dublin, the
centre of English rule in Ireland, the O'Tooles maintained
a fierce independence and, together with their
neighbours and occasional allies the O'Byrnes, were a
source of great fear to the inhabitants of Dublin and the
Pale for almost four centuries. It was only in the

O'TOOLE

seventeenth century, with the final and general collapse of Gaelic power, that the O'Tooles were 'pacified', as the English put it.

Unlike most of the other Gaelic aristocracy, however, the line of the O'Tooles survived intact; there were two branches, of Powerscourt and Castle Kevin, both in Wicklow. Descendants of the former are living in Wicklow and in the U.S. The representatives of the latter have lived in France for many generations.

The most famous bearer of the name is undoubtedly St Laurence O'Toole, a member of the leading O'Toole family who became abbot of the monastery of Glendalough at the age of 25, and was chosen by the people and clergy as first Archbishop of Dublin in 1162. He subsequently led the resistance and negotiation with the Norman invaders.

PATTERSON

Patterson is now found throughout Ireland, though it is common only in Ulster, being particularly frequent in Co. Down. Originally it is a Lowland Scottish name, meaning, simply, 'Patrick's son', and was also used as an anglicisation of the Highland Gaelic surname, *Mac (Gille) Phádraig*, meaning 'son of the follower of Patrick'. In addition, there is a surname, *Mac Pháidín*, from *Páidín*, a diminutive of Patrick, which arose separately in both Ulster and Scotland, and which has been anglicised as Patterson, as well as the more usual (Mc)Fadden and (Mc)Padden. The founder of the Belfast Natural History Society was Robert Patterson (1802-1872).

POWER

Power is originally a Norman name, which may derive from the Old French *povre*, meaning 'poor', or from *pohier*, meaning a native of the town of *Pois* in Picardy in France, so called from the Old French *pois*, meaning 'fish', a name given it because of its rivers. The surname is also found in Ireland as 'Le Poer', and in the Irish version 'de Paor'. The first Norman settlers of the name were in Co. Waterford, where members of the family retained large estates up to the nineteenth century, and the surname is still most numerous by far in that county, although it has also spread into the adjoining

POWER

counties of Kilkenny, Cork, Tipperary and Wexford. The family which founded Power's distillery, famous for its whiskey, were from Wexford, with their seat at Edermine, near Enniscorthy.

QUIGLEY

Quigley is the principal English version of the Irish *Ó Coigligh*, from *coigleach*, meaning 'unkempt'. The main origin of the family was in in Co. Mayo, where they were part of the powerful *Uí Fiachrach* tribal grouping. From there they were dispersed at an early date, principally to the adjacent territories now part of counties Sligo, Donegal and Derry, where the name is principally found today. There appears also to have been a separate *Ó Coigligh* family which arose in Co. Wexford, where the

QUIGLEY

QUINN

name has been anglicised for the most part as 'Cogley', although Quigley is also frequent.

QUINN

Quinn is now one of the most numerous of Irish surnames, among the twenty most common, and is to be found throughout the country. The name arose separately in four distinct areas. In three of these – near the modern town of Corofin in Co. Clare, in the glens of north Antrim, and in Co. Longford – the Irish original from which the surname derives is *Ó Coinn*, from *Conn*, a popular personal name meaning 'chief' or 'leader'. The most notable of these families is that based in Clare, where the barony of Inchiquin bears their name; in early times they were chiefs of the Clan Heffernan, and their descendants are today Earls of Dunraven and Mountearl.

The fourth area is Tyrone, where the surname is today the most common in the county. Here the individual from whom descent is claimed was *Coinne*, a great-great-grandson of Niall of the Nine Hostages, the fifth-century monarch who founded the dynasty of the *Uí Néill*. In the fighting forces of the O'Neills, the *Ó Coinne* were traditionally quartermasters.

REDMOND

Redmond is a Norman surname, derived from the personal name Raymond or Raimund, which is made up of the Germanic roots *ragin* 'counsel', and *mund*, 'protection'. The first of the name in Ireland was Alexander Redmond (or 'FitzRedmond'), who was granted the Hook area of Co. Wexford in the first wave of the Norman settlement. The descent of the senior

REDMOND

lines of this family is very well documented down to the twentieth century, while the junior lines have flourished and multiplied, to the point where Redmond is now an extremely common name in the county. Other branches have now also established themselves throughout Ireland. There is also a native Irish family of Co. Wexford, the MacDavymores, who adopted the surname of Redmond in the early seventeenth century, taking it from Redmond MacDavymore. This family were a branch of the powerful MacMurroughs, and were based in the north of the county, while the Norman Redmonds are most strongly associated with south Wexford, where they first settled. The most famous bearer of the name was John Redmond (1855-1918), leader of the Irish Party in the British House of Commons until the party was eclipsed by the rise of *Sinn Féin*.

REGAN

Regan, along with its variants Reagan and O'Re(a)gan, comes from the Irish *Ó Ríagáin*, perhaps from *ríodhgach*, meaning 'impulsive' or 'angry'. It originated independently in at least three different areas. In the Meath/Dublin region it was borne by one of the Four Tribes of Tara, who migrated to Co. Laois, where their descendants are still to be found. A second family claims descent from Riagán, a nephew of the eleventh-century High King Brian Boru; their homeland was the historic kingdom of Thomond, in what is now Co. Limerick. East Cork, around the modern town of Fermoy, was the original territory of the third family of *Ó Ríagáin*. Their influence in the wider area of east Cork is recorded in the townland names of Coolyregan in Brigown parish, and two Ballyregans, in the parishes of Cloyne and Carrigtohill. By the sixteenth century most members of this family had migrated to the southwest, however, and it is with west Cork that the name is most strongly linked today.

REID

Reid, with its variants Reed and Read(e), is now one of the 100 most common surnames in Ireland. In form it is English, and can derive from a nickname for someone who is red-haired or ruddy (from the Old English *read*),

REGAN

RIORDAN

from a name for someone who lived in a clearing in a wood (Old English *ried*), or from the various places in England called Read or similar. No doubt many bearing the name in Ireland are of English stock. In addition, a number of Scots Gaelic surnames – MacRory, Ruaidh ('red'), and MacInroy – were frequently anglicised Reid, and many Reids in Ulster especially are descended from Scottish settlers. However, there were also two Gaelic families, the *Ó Maoildeirg* ('Mulderrig' – 'red chieftain') of Mayo and Antrim, and the *Ó Maoilbhríghde* ('Mulreedy' – 'devotee of St Brigid') of Co. Roscommon,

whose surnames have often been anglicised Reid, by semi-translation and abbreviation respectively. Nano Reid (1905-1981) was one of the best known Irish painters of her generation, celebrated for her skilful evocation of the landscape of her native Co. Louth.

REILLY

Reilly, with its variants Riley and (O')R(e)ily, comes from the Irish *Ó Raghallaigh*, and is extremely common

even in the twelfth century, the *Ó Rioghbhárdáin* migrated south to Co. Cork, where they settled in the west of the county, in Muskerry particularly, and the strength of their association with this part of the country remains remarkable; a large majority of those bearing the name originate in Co. Cork. Seán Ó Riordáin (1916-1971), born in Ballyvourney, Co. Cork, is considered by many to have been the finest Irish-language poet of the twentieth century.

ROBINSON

Robinson is one of the 100 most common surnames in Ireland. In form it is English, from Robin, a diminutive of Robert, though it is also common in Scotland, where in many cases it has been used as a synonym of Robertson, a surname used by the Clan Donnachie. Many Robinsons in Ulster, where the name is among the twenty most common, will be of this connection. The majority elsewhere are almost certainly of English stock. The best-known contemporary bearer of the name is undoubtedly Mary Robinson (*née* Bourke), who was elected President of Ireland in 1990. Before her election she was already widely respected as a constitutional lawyer and human rights campaigner.

ROCHE

Roche, together with its variants Roach, Roch, etc, is a name of Norman origin. Although the obvious derivation is from the French *roche*, 'rock', the earliest bearer of the surname in Ireland, Richard FitzGodebert de la Roche, in fact adopted the surname after his place of origin in Wales, Rhos in Pembrokeshire. He was one of the first Norman arrivals, coming in 1167, and acquiring with others of his family large tracts of south Co. Wexford. Over the centuries the family became thoroughly hibernicized, to the point where they were prominent in the many rebellions against English rule, the best-known being Father Philip Roche, who led the Irish in the Battle of Horetown in 1798. The name is still strongly linked with Co. Wexford, where a townland of Rochestown exists today, but over the centuries many of the family migrated south, particularly to the area around the modern town of Fermoy in Co. Cork, where

REILLY

and widespread throughout Ireland. It originated in the old kingdom of Breffny, which included areas now in counties Cavan and Longford, where the O'Reillys were long the dominant family. Their prosperity may be gauged by the fact the 'reilly' was at one point a colloquial term for money in Ireland. After the collapse of Gaelic power in the seventeenth century large numbers emigrated to serve in the armies of France, many in Colonel Edmund O'Reilly's regiment of foot. The connection with the original homeland is still strong, however; even today (O')Reilly is the single most numerous surname in both Cavan and Longford.

RIORDAN

Riordan, with its variants O'Riordan and Reardan, comes from the Irish original *Ó Rioghbhárdáin* (*Ó Ríordáin* in modern Irish), *riogh-* meaning 'royal', and *bárdán* a diminutive of *bard*, 'poet'. The surname originated in the area between the modern towns of Thurles in Co. Tipperary and Birr in Co. Offaly. Very early, perhaps

ROCHE   RYAN

they prospered greatly. They also spread further afield and multiplied throughout the southern province of Munster; Roche is today one of the commonest surnames in that area.

ROGERS

Rogers is one of the most common surnames in Britain and Ireland. Its English origin is simple: it means 'son of Roger', a very common personal name made up of two Germanic elements: *hrod,* 'renown' and *geri,* 'spear'. It is also common in Scotland, where it is frequently spelt Rodgers. Many, if not most of those bearing the name in Ireland are of English and Scottish descent. However, the Gaelic Irish surname *Mac Ruaidhrí,* from the personal name Ruaidhri, meaning 'red king', was also anglicised as Rogers. Two *Mac Ruaidhrí* families are notable in early times, one based in Co. Tyrone, a branch of whom migrated north to Co. Derry, the other in Co. Fermanagh, possibly an offshoot of the Maguires. In these areas the surname was also anglicised MacRory and MacCrory.

In addition, because Ruaidhrí was such a common personal name, many individuals in the sixteenth and seventeenth centuries were identified by the fathers' names. A son of Ruaidhrí Ó Briain might, for example, be known as Mac Ruaidhrí Ó Briain. In a significant number of cases the Mac Ruaidhri was then passed on to the next generation, instead of Ó Briain, becoming an hereditary surname in its own right, and was then anglicised 'Rogers'.

ROONEY

Rooney is the anglicised version of *Ó Ruanaidh,* from Ruanadh, a personal name meaning 'champion'. The principal family of the name originated in Co. Down, where their territory was centred on the parish of Ballyroney, which includes their name. They have produced many poets, the most recent of whom is Pádraig Rooney, winner of the Kavanagh Prize for Poetry in 1986. Two other families, both from Co. Fermanagh, have also anglicised their surnames as Rooney, the *Ó*

Maolruanaidh ('Mulrooney'), and the *Mac Maolruanaidh* ('Macarooney'), both prominent in the early history of the county.

RYAN

Ryan is today one of the commonest surnames in Ireland. Unlike many other common surnames, however, it has one major origin, in the family of *Ó Maoilriaghain*, meaning 'descendant of a devotee of St Riaghan'. The anglicisation 'Mulryan' began to fade as early as the seventeenth century, and is today virtually unknown apart from a few pockets in counties Galway and Leitrim, possibly derived from a different family. The surname first appears in the fourteenth century in the barony of Owney, on the borders of counties Limerick and Tipperary, where the *Ó Maoilriaghain* displaced the O'Heffernans. Even today the surname is highly concentrated in this area. In Carlow and adjoining areas Ryan may also derive from *Ó Riaghain*, sometimes confused with Regan. Patrick J. Ryan (1883-1964) emigrated to the U.S., won a gold medal for hammer-throwing for that country in the 1920 Olympics, and then returned to farming in Pallasgreen in Limerick.

SCOTT

Scott is a very common surname in Ireland, and is particularly numerous in Ulster. It derives ultimately from the Latin *Scottus* which, confusingly, means 'Irishman'. After the Irish colonization of that country in the sixth century, 'Scotland' eventually became the English name for the territory controlled by the Gaelic-speaking descendants of the settlers, more or less the Highlands. In the course of time, by extension, the name was applied to all of what we now know as Scotland. 'Scott' as a descriptive name was initially used for the Highlanders but, like the name of the country, in the end came to refer to all Scots. A Lowland Scottish family, based along the Borders, are in fact the forbears of many Ulster bearers of the name. They were one of the notorious 'riding clans', many of whose members settled in Fermanagh in the seventeenth century after their power was broken by James II. Johannes Scottus Eriugena (*c.*180-877), the philosopher and theologian, appears on the Irish £5 note. His work was not uncontroversial: *De Praedestinatione* was condemned at the Council of Valence in 855 as *pultes Scottorum*, 'Irish porridge', and his major work, *De Divisione Naturae*, was repeatedly condemned and finally placed on the Papal Index in 1685.

SHEEHAN

Sheehan is the anglicisation of the Irish *Ó Síodhacháin*, from a diminutive of *síodhach*, meaning 'peaceful'. The principal family of the name were part of the *Dál gCais*, the tribal grouping occupying an area now in counties Limerick and Clare which produced Brian Boru, High King of Ireland in the eleventh century. Some of the traditional genealogies have the descent of the Sheehans

SHEEHAN

from one Sidhechan, a contemporary of Brian Boru and distantly related to him. Initially they appear to have lived in the south of Co. Limerick, in the barony of Connello. In very early times, however, they migrated south, into the northeast of the present Co. Cork, where

they are still most numerous. Over the course of the centuries, large numbers have also migrated into Co. Kerry, while a significant number also remained in their homeland of Limerick. In these areas, the surname is very common indeed.

SHERIDAN

Sheridan is the English version of *Ó Sirideáin*, from the personal name *Sirideán*, which is possibly related to *sirigh*, 'to seek'. The surname arose in the modern Co. Longford, where the *Ó Sirideáin* held hereditary church offices and land in the parish of Granard. They later moved to the adjoining county of Cavan, where they became followers of the rulers of Breffny, the O'Reillys. Cavan is still the area in which the surname is most common, though it has now spread throughout the northern half of the country. The most famous bearer of the name was the playwright Richard Brinsley Sheridan (1751-1817), born in Dublin, whose three masterpieces, *The Rivals*, *The School for Scandal* and *The Critic* display brilliant comic invention.

SMITH

Smith is a surname famous for being ordinary; it is the most common name in England, Scotland, Wales and Ulster, while it is the fifth most common in Ireland as a whole. Antrim and Cavan are the areas in which it is most numerous. Its English origin, designating an armourer, smith or farrier, and many bearing the name, in Ulster especially, will be of English stock. The Scottish originals anglicised as Smith are *Mac Gobha* and *Mac Gobhann*, both meaning 'son of the smith'. These were also anglicised phonetically as (Mac)Gow and (Mac)Gowan. At least two major families of the name are recorded, branches of the Clan Donald and the Clan MacPherson. The principal Irish name is *Mac Gabhainn*, also 'son of the smith', and is strongly rooted in Co. Cavan, where the *Mac Gabhainn* were one of the most powerful families. The vast majority of the family in Cavan anglicised their name to Smith. Among less prominent families adopting Smith were the *Ó Gabhainn* ('O'Gowan') of Drummully in Fermanagh and of Co. Down, and the *Mac an Gabhan* of Ballymagowan in Co. Tyrone.

SHERIDAN

SWEENEY

STEWART

Although coming among the top sixty in the list of the most common names in Ireland as a whole, Stewart or Stuart is to be found almost exclusively in Ulster, where it is of Scottish origin. The surname is occupational, referring to an administrative official (modern English 'steward'), and this word derives from a compound of the two Old English terms *stig*, 'house', and *weard*, 'guardian'. The surname arose in various locations in Scotland, no doubt due to the fact that every local lord and bishop would have his own steward. Its popularity as a surname was also influenced by the royal family, the Stuarts, who ruled Scotland from 1371 to 1603, and Scotland and England from then until 1688. They were hereditary High Stewards of Scotland for six generations before they acquired the throne, and this is the source of their surname. The spelling 'Stuart' is the French version of the name, popularised in the sixteenth century by Mary, Queen of Scots, who was educated in France.

SWEENEY

Sweeney, along with its variants MacSweeny and MacSwiney, comes from the Irish *Mac Suibhne*, from *suibhne*, meaning 'pleasant'. The original *Suibhne* from whom the surname derives was a Scottish chief based in Argyle around the year 1200. His people were of mixed Viking and Irish descent, and their fame as fighters meant that they were much in demand in Ireland as gallowglasses, or mercenaries. Suibhne's great-great-grandson Muchadh Maer Mac Suibhne settled in the Fanad district of the modern Co. Donegal in the fourteenth century, and his offspring soon split into distinct groups, the principal ones being *Mac Suibhne Fanad* and *Mac Suibhne na dTuath*. For over three centuries, up to the final defeat of the seventeenth century, they fought as gallowglasses in the struggles of Ulster, mainly on behalf of the O'Donnells. Members of both groups also made their way south to Cork in the late fifteenth century and served the MacCarthys, acquiring territory of their own in Muskerry. The Cork family prospered and multiplied, and today the surname is more numerous in the Cork/Kerry area than in its original Irish homeland of Ulster.

TOBIN

TOBIN

Tobin is in Irish *Tóibín*, which is a Gaelicised version of the Norman 'St Aubin', after the place of the same name in Brittany, so called from the dedication of its church to St Albin. The family came to Ireland in the immediate aftermath of the Norman invasion, and by the early thirteenth century were well established in counties Kilkenny and Tipperary; their power in the latter county is attested by the (unofficial) title 'Baron of Coursey', by which the head of the family was known in the Middle Ages. In the course of time the surname also spread into the adjoining counties of Cork and Waterford, and this is the area in which it remains most common by far today. The two best-known contemporary bearers of the name in Ireland are the comic actor Niall Tóibín and the novelist and poet Colm Tóibín.

WALLACE

Wallace comes from the Anglo-Norman French *le waleis*, meaning simply 'the foreigner' or 'the stranger', which was used in different parts of Britain to denote Scots, Welsh or Breton origin, strangeness obviously being in the eye of the beholder. In medieval Ireland the name was generally used to mean 'the Welshman', and arrived in the wake of the Norman invasion; the first Norman invaders came from Wales. The surname became, and remains, numerous in the major urban centres of population: Dublin, Cork, Limerick and Galway. It is most numerous, however, in Ulster, where bearers will generally be of Scottish descent. In Scotland the name was more usually applied to descendants of the small pocket of Strathclyde Britons who survived into the Middle Ages. This was the origin of Scotland's national hero, Sir William Wallace. The best-known Irish bearer of the name was the composer William Vincent Wallace (1812-1865), who became world famous after the success of his operas *Maritana*, and *Lurline*.

WALSH

Walsh is among the five most numerous surnames in Ireland, found throughout the country, with particular concentrations in Connacht in counties Mayo and Galway, in Munster in counties Cork and Waterford, and in Leinster in counties Kilkenny and Wexford. It is a semi-translation of the Irish surname *Breathnach*, meaning 'British' or 'Welsh', also sometimes anglicised as 'Brannagh'. The surname thus has the same historical origin as Wallace, but arrived at its present form by a more circuitous route. Unlike most of the other Hiberno-Norman families, such as the Burkes, the Fitzgeralds etc., who can trace their ancestry to a small number of known individuals, the Walshes have many different origins, since the name arose independently in many different places, for obvious reasons. Two exceptions should perhaps be mentioned: the descendants of Haylen Brenach, one of those who arrived in 1172, became very well known and prosperous in the south and east of the country, while 'Walynus', who arrived in 1169, is said to have been the progenitor of the Walshes of Tirawley in Co. Mayo, and the brother of Barrett, the ancestor of the Barretts of the same county.

WARD

Ward is common and widespread throughout Ireland, England and Wales. In Britain it is generally an occupational surname, derived from the Old English *weard*, meaning 'guard'. Some in Ireland may be of English stock, as, for example, in the case of the family who now hold the title of Viscounts Bangor in Co. Down. In the vast majority of cases, however, Ward in Ireland is the anglicisation of *Mac an Bháird*, meaning 'son of the poet (bard)'; the equivalent Scottish surname almost always became 'Baird'. Two families are historically prominent, one based near the modern town of Ballinasloe in Co Galway, and the other near Glenties in Co. Donegal. Both families were professional hereditary poets, as their surname implies, to the O'Kellys and the O'Donnells respectively. A branch of the northern family also became poets to the O'Neills in Co. Tyrone. Today the largest single concentrations of the surname are to be found in the original homelands, counties Galway and Donegal.

WHELAN

Whelan, along with its common variant Phelan, comes from the Irish *Ó Faoláin*, from a diminutive of *faol*, 'wolf'. Taken together, the two names come among the fifty most numerous in Ireland. The family originated in the ancient kingdom of Decies, part of the modern county of Waterford, where they were rulers up to the Norman invasion. From this centre the surname has now spread to the adjoining counties of Kilkenny, Cork, Wexford and, further north, Carlow. It is also to be found throughout the country, however. The best known modern bearer of the name was Seán Ó Faoláin, the novelist and short story writer, whose writing career spanned six decades. His family name was originally Whelan. His daughter Julia is also a distinguished novelist.

WHITE

White is of the most common surnames in England, Wales, Scotland and Ireland. In England its most common origin is as a descriptive nickname for someone who was fair-haired or pale, and a sizable proportion of

WALSH

WHELAN

those bearing the name in Ireland will be of English extraction; such families were prominent in Clare, Waterford and Kilkenny. In some cases, as families were absorbed by Gaelic culture, White was phonetically hibernicized *Mac Faoite*. After the final collapse of the Gaelic order in the seventeenth century this was re-anglicised as MacWhitty and MacQuitty, as well as the original White. In the north of Ireland, many Whites are of Scottish extraction. The surname was a semi-translation of the Highland Gaelic *Mac Gille Bháin*, 'son of the fair-haired servant or youth', and was also adopted by many of the MacGregors and Lamonts when they were outlawed and their own names proscribed. Elsewhere in Ireland White was sometimes used locally for many Irish originals containing, or thought to contain, the elements *bán* ('white') or *fionn* ('fair')

WOODS

In appearance at least, Woods, together with Wood, is of course an English name, denoting a person who lived near a wood or, in some cases, a woodcutter. In Ireland, however, the majority of those bearing the surname are of native Irish extraction. The Irish for a wood is *coill*, plural *coillte*, and many Irish names containing elements which sounded similar in untutored English ears were mistranslated as 'Woods'. Among such names are: *Mac Giolla Comhghaill* ('MacIlhoyle'/'Coyle'), 'son of the follower of St Comall', found in Donegal and Monaghan; *Mac an Choiligh* ('MacQuilly'/'Magilly'), 'son of the cock', from Co. Roscommon; *Mac Giolla Chomghain* ('MacElhone'), 'son of the follower of St Comgan' in Co. Tyrone, and *Mac Caoilte* ('Quilty') in Munster. The only family whose surname actually did contain *coill* were the *Mac Conchoille*, 'son of the hound of the woods', who were also anglicised phonetically as MacEnhill. They were based near Omagh in Co. Tyrone. The form Woods is more than ten times commoner in Ireland than in England and Wales.

The Caragh River, near Glenbeigh in Co. Kerry. There is an intimate
link between the Irish countryside and the Irish character.

Clans and Families of Ireland

Index

Islands off the Atlantic coast of Kerry

Clans and Families of Ireland

Picture Credits

The Bettmann Archive: 52 (left), 129 (top); **Bord Failte/Irish Tourist Board:** 16 (bottom), 25 (top and bottom left), 94 (top); **British Library:** 39; **Michael Diggin:** 8, 13, 16 (top), 19, 20, 27, 33, 54, 67, 68, 86 (bottom), 109, 140 (right), 159, 161 (bottom), 184; **Mary Evans Picture Library:** 42, 43, 48; **The Institute of Texan Cultures, San Antonio, Texas:** 66; **Stella Johnson:** 62; **Lotherton Hall (Leeds City Art Gallery):** 47; **The Library Company of Philadelphia:** 53; **Library of Congress, Washington, D.C.:** 64, 65; **The Mansell Collection:** 56; **The National Gallery of Ireland:** 36 (top); **The New York Historical Society:** 61; **Picturepoint, London:** 22, 26 (bottom), 46; **Tony Ruta, New York:** 35; **The Slide File:** 105 (left); **The State Heraldic Museum:** 116; **Don Sutton International Photo Library:** 17, 21, 36 (bottom), 50-51; **All other photographs Neil Sutherland/Colour Library Books Ltd Heraldic device artwork by Myra Maguire**

Clans and Families of Ireland

Acknowledgements

The author and publishers would like to thank all the individuals and organisations who provided advice and assistance throughout the preparation of this book. Special thanks are due to Donal Begley, Chief Herald of Ireland, the Genealogical Office, and to the Genealogical Museum, Dublin, for granting permission to photograph items from their collection.